Comments about the first edition of
WHATEVER HAPPENED TO JUSTICE?

"This is a wonderfully readable and interesting book about the legal principles which undergird a free society. Richard Maybury challenges the reader to explore the inextricable connections between law and economics, and between economic and political liberty. I can think of no more important subject, and I highly recommend this lucid and thoughtful volume."

—William E. Simon
former U.S. Treasury Secretary
President, John M. Olin Foundation

"Richard Maybury's *Whatever Happened to Justice?* is critical reading for all Americans. If our economic and political downfall is to be avoided, we must expose an entire generation of Americans to the ideas found in this wonderful book."

—Ron Paul
member of Congress

"Mr. Maybury has done an outstanding job of reminding us of the origin of common law and its vital importance to the preservation of freedom."

—Don Rogers
California State Senator

"Every lawyer should wonder 'Whatever Happened to Justice?' Maybury's book indicts statism in our courtrooms and renders a verdict of guilty beyond any reasonable doubt. His work is a Corpus Juris Naturalis!"

—Ellis Rexwood Curry, IV
Attorney at Law

"There is a naked clarity to Maybury's thought that washes over the reader like cleansing rain. His examination of the dynamics of common law is brilliant. As a teacher for all ages, Mr. Maybury is a virtuoso. Bravo!"

—John Taylor Gatto
former New York State Teacher of the Year
3X New York City Teacher of the Year
author, DUMBING US DOWN

"WHATEVER HAPPENED TO PENNY CANDY? initiated, and WHATEVER HAPPENED TO JUSTICE? seconds Maybury's nomination to sit beside Bastiat and Hazlitt in the Good Explainers Hall of Fame."

—Marshall Fritz
President, Pioneer Christian Academy

"We are drowning in an ocean of crazy laws and litigation. This book is a life preserver, a reminder of the fundamental rules which are needed for a free society."

—Karl Hess
author, CAPITALISM FOR KIDS
former U.S. Presidential speechwriter
former Associate Editor of NEWSWEEK

"The author of WHATEVER HAPPENED TO PENNY CANDY? has done even better with WHATEVER HAPPENED TO JUSTICE? Maybury has a gift for translating what sounds like tedious information into very personalized examples. He follows the PENNY CANDY format, where Uncle Eric is writing to...Chris. Each letter is reasonably brief, so students will not be overwhelmed with too much information at once. Use this book as a supplement to American history or government studies. It will not take much time to read through, although it might generate lengthy discussions. No matter what else you use, this book is a must! Highly recommended for reading and discussion."

—Cathy Duffy
author, CHRISTIAN HOME EDUCATORS' CURRICULUM MANUAL

"Unless we return to the principles of common and natural law, America is headed for totalitarianism. Richard Maybury's book will bring us back from the brink and restore freedom and responsibility to this great nation."
—Mark Skousen, editor, FORECASTS & STRATEGIES

"Richard Maybury is one of my favorite people. All of his writing is clear and direct. Most important—it's philosophically uncompromising. If you want the answers to how a truly free society would solve the problems of poverty, pollution, drugs, consumer protection, and the like, this book has them. If you're looking for a worthwhile gift for a young person especially, give this book."

—Doug Casey
editor, CRISIS INVESTING

"WHATEVER HAPPENED TO JUSTICE? is an important book. Maybury explains how civilization depends on shared common values of right and wrong—how a revival of the Common Law would strengthen those values and reverse the destructive trends of modern society. The common sense approach of this book makes it an excellent tool for introducing these ideas to children."

—Philip Martin Koehne
President, KDF, Inc.
author, THE CULT OF LEGISLATION

An Uncle Eric Book

Whatever Happened to Justice?

Revised Edition

by Richard J. Maybury
(Uncle Eric)

published by
Bluestocking Press
www.BluestockingPress.com

About the Uncle Eric Series

The Uncle Eric series of books is written by Richard J. Maybury for young and old alike. Using the epistolary style of writing (using letters to tell a story), Mr. Maybury plays the part of an economist writing a series of letters to his niece or nephew. Using stories and examples, he gives interesting and clear explanations of topics that are generally thought to be too difficult for anyone but experts.

Mr. Maybury warns, "beware of anyone who tells you a topic is above you or better left to experts. Many people are twice as smart as they think they are, but they've been intimidated into believing some topics are above them. You can understand almost anything if it is explained well."

The series is called UNCLE ERIC'S MODEL OF HOW THE WORLD WORKS. In the series, Mr. Maybury writes from the political, legal, and economic viewpoint of America's Founders. The books can be read in any order, and have been written to stand alone. To get the most from each one, however, Mr. Maybury suggests the following order of reading:

Uncle Eric's Model
of How the World Works

Uncle Eric Talks About Personal, Career, and Financial Security

Whatever Happened to Penny Candy?

Whatever Happened to Justice?

Are You Liberal? Conservative? or Confused?

Ancient Rome: How It Affects You Today

Evaluating Books: What Would Thomas Jefferson Think About This?

The Money Mystery

The Clipper Ship Strategy

The Thousand Year War in the Mideast

World War I: The Rest of the Story and How It Affects You Today

World War II: The Rest of the Story and How It Affects You Today

(Study guides available or forthcoming for above titles.)

Quantity Discounts Available

The Uncle Eric books are available at special quantity discounts for bulk purchases to individuals, businesses, schools, libraries, and associations, to be distributed as gifts, premiums, or as fund raisers.

For terms and discount schedule contact:

Special Sales Department
Bluestocking Press
Phone: 800-959-8586
email: CustomerService@BluestockingPress.com
web site: www.BluestockingPress.com

Specify how books are to be distributed: for classrooms, or as gifts, premiums, fund raisers — or to be resold.

Cover Design by Brian C. Williams, El Dorado, CA
Cover Illustration by Bob O'Hara, Georgetown, CA
Edited by Jane A. Williams

Printed and bound in the United States of America.

Library of Congress Cataloging-in-Publication Data
Maybury, Rick.
    Whatever happened to justice? / by Richard J. Maybury (Uncle Eric).--Rev. ed.
        p.   cm. -- (An Uncle Eric book)
    Includes bibliographical references and index.
    ISBN-13: 978-0-942617-46-7 (soft cover : alk. paper)
    ISBN-10:   0-942617-46-0 (soft cover : alk. paper)
    1. Justice, Administration of--United States. 2. Law--Philosophy.
    I. Title. II. Series.

KF384.Z9M39 2004
340'.11--dc22   2004002422

Printed by McNaughton & Gunn, Inc.
Saline, MI USA
(October 2009)
Published by Bluestocking Press • P.O. Box 1014
Placerville, CA 95667-1014
web site: www.BluestockingPress.com

This book is dedicated to three people.

To Marilyn.
Without her support,
little of my writing would exist.

To my parents.
They taught that right and wrong
are not matters of opinion.

Disclaimer

This book is designed to provide information in regard to the subject matter covered. It is sold with the understanding that the publisher and author are not engaged in rendering legal or other professional services. If legal or other expert assistance is required, the services of a competent professional should be sought.

Every effort has been made to make this book as complete and as accurate as possible. However, there may be mistakes both typographical and in content. Therefore, this text should be used as a general guide.

The purpose of this book is to educate. The author, Bluestocking Press, and any and all persons or entities involved in any way in the preparation, publication, sale, or distribution of this book disclaim all responsibility for the legal effects or consequences of any document prepared or action taken in reliance upon any information contained in this book. No representations, either expressed or implied, are made or given regarding the legal consequences of the use of any information contained in this book. You have the responsibility to check all material you read here before relying on it. The author and Bluestocking Press shall have neither liability nor responsibility to any person or entity with respect to any loss or damage caused, or alleged to be caused, directly or indirectly by the information contained in this book.

If you do not wish to be bound by the above you may return this book to the publisher for a full refund.

.

Contents

Study Guide Available

BLUESTOCKING GUIDE: JUSTICE

by Kathryn Daniels

— based on Richard J. Maybury's book —
WHATEVER HAPPENED TO JUSTICE?

This Bluestocking Guide is designed to enhance the student's understanding and retention of the subject matter presented, and includes: 1) chapter-by-chapter comprehension questions and answers, 2) application exercises and questions to guide students in applying the concepts learned to everyday life, 3) research activities, 4) essay assignments, 5) thought questions to facilitate student-teacher discussion, and 6) a final exam.

Order from your favorite book store or direct from the publisher: Bluestocking Press (see order information on last page of this book).

Study Guides
are available or forthcoming
for other Uncle Eric books.

Note to Reader

Throughout the book when a word that appears in the glossary is introduced in the text, it is displayed in **bold typeface**.

Author's Disclosure

For reasons I do not understand, writers today are supposed to be objective. Few disclose the viewpoints or opinions they use to decide what information is important and what is not, or what shall be presented or omitted.

I do not adhere to this standard and make no pretense of being objective. I am biased in favor of liberty, free markets, and international neutrality and proud of it. So I disclose my viewpoint, which you will find explained in detail in my other books.[1]

For those who have not yet read these publications, I call my viewpoint Juris Naturalism (pronounced *jur*-es *nach*-e-re-liz-em, sometimes abbreviated JN) meaning the belief in a natural law that is higher than any government's law. Here are six quotes from America's Founders that help to describe this viewpoint:

> ...all men are created equal, that they are endowed by their Creator with certain unalienable rights.
> — Declaration of Independence, 1776

> The natural rights of the colonists are these: first, a right to life; second to liberty; third to property; together with the right to support and defend them in the best manner they can.
> — Samuel Adams, 1772

---

[1] For a list of Uncle Eric books by Richard Maybury see page four of this book. Uncle Eric books are published by Bluestocking Press, phone: 800-959-8586, web site: www.BluestockingPress.com

It is strangely absurd to suppose that a million of human beings collected together are not under the same moral laws which bind each of them separately.
— Thomas Jefferson, 1816

A wise and frugal government, which shall restrain men from injuring one another, which shall leave them otherwise free to regulate their own pursuits of industry and improvement, and shall not take from the mouth of labor the bread it has earned. This is the sum of good government.
— Thomas Jefferson, 1801

Not a place on earth might be so happy as America. Her situation is remote from all the wrangling world, and she has nothing to do but to trade with them.
— Thomas Paine, 1776

The great rule of conduct for us, in regard to foreign nations, is, in extending our commercial relations, to have with them as little political connection as possible.
— George Washington, 1796

George
Washington

About Richard J. Maybury

Richard Maybury, also known as Uncle Eric, is a world renowned author, lecturer, and geopolitical analyst. He consults with business firms in the U.S. and Europe. Richard is the former Global Affairs editor of MONEYWORLD and widely regarded as one of the finest free-market writers in America. Mr. Maybury's articles have appeared in THE WALL STREET JOURNAL, USA TODAY, and other major publications.

Richard Maybury has penned eleven books in the Uncle Eric series. His books have been endorsed by top business leaders including former U.S. Treasury Secretary William Simon, and he has been interviewed on more than 250 radio and TV shows across America.

He has been married for more than 35 years, has lived abroad, traveled around the world, and visited 48 states and 40 countries.

He is truly a teacher for all ages.

Author's Introduction
To Help The Young

We older generations never had to face what the young are facing. America's wonderful liberty and abundance are slipping away. Free markets are disappearing. Opportunity has diminished and poverty is growing.

Until the 1970s, each generation of Americans expected to do better than any who came before. No more. Statistics confirm that our children are the first Americans ever to have little chance of living as well as their parents. If the drift away from free markets continues, they may not even live as long, and our grandchildren certainly won't.

Many free market advocates assume that if Americans can be taught enough economics they will again become dedicated to free markets; the downhill slide will be reversed. Educational efforts are under way to achieve this, but I'm afraid they won't be enough.

Teaching economics is important, but by itself it will not revive support for free markets.

To my knowledge, not once in all of history has any nation, including America, acquired a free market through the people's understanding of free markets.

A long ignored key point in American history is that Adam Smith's seminal economic analysis WEALTH OF NATIONS was not published until 1776.

This means economics at the time of the American Revolution was a fledgling science. The exact reasons why free markets are so effective in eliminating poverty and creating abundance were still unclear.

Yet America became the most free and prosperous land ever known.

How did people who did not understand economics know to create free markets?

They didn't, but they were dedicated to the principles of the old common law.

When these elementary legal principles are widely obeyed, free markets spring up automatically. Even if the people have no knowledge of economics whatsoever—even if they cannot read—a free market develops, it's automatic.

The world seems to be constructed in such a way that liberty and abundance become widespread when ethical behavior becomes widespread. The two fundamental principles of common law are a part of the fabric of the universe. Disobey them and life gets worse; obey and life gets better.

Observe Hong Kong. For more than a half-century, until the Red Chinese government took it over in 1997, Hong Kong was a magnet for Red China's impoverished victims of **socialism**. It was often cited as a model of free market effectiveness, one of the most prosperous cities in Asia. Yet most in Hong Kong know nothing of free market economics. The city's legal system just happened to be based on British common law principles.[2]

We must revive the American people's dedication to the basic principles of the old common law. In this book I've summarized these basics into a simple formula of 17 words. These 17 words are a recipe for reversing America's decline and giving the young the opportunities we had.

Once the people become dedicated to this formula, free markets will be revived. It's automatic.

— Richard J. Maybury

---

[2] Until Red China took over Hong Kong in 1997.

"At what point shall we expect the approach of danger? By what means shall we fortify against it?

"Shall we expect some transatlantic military giant to step the ocean and crush us at a blow? Never! All the armies of Europe, Asia and Africa combined, with all the treasure of the earth (our own excepted) in their military chest, with Bonaparte for a commander, could not by force, take a drink from the Ohio, or make a track on the Blue Ridge, in a trial of a thousand years.

"At what point then is the approach of danger to be expected? I answer, if it ever reaches us, it must spring up amongst us. It cannot come from abroad. If destruction be our lot, we must ourselves be its author and finisher. As a nation of free men, we must live through all time, or die by suicide."

— Abraham Lincoln

Some ideas are considered dangerous, and you have been protected from hearing them. Are you happy about this?

"Percentage of Americans in a 1990 poll who said the Ku Klux Klan and Communist Party should not enjoy freedom of speech: 35."

— U.S. NEWS & WORLD REPORT

"I tolerate with the utmost latitude the right of others to differ from me in opinion."

— Thomas Jefferson

1

The Cause Is Law

"Bodily exercise, when compulsory, does no harm to the body; But knowledge which is acquired under compulsion obtains no hold on the mind."

— *Plato, circa 400 B.C.*

Dear Chris,

Thanks for your recent phone call. Exchanging letters[3] about **economics** was fun for me, too. I'm glad you enjoyed my stories about inflation, investment cycles, and recessions. I'm sure you'll someday find them useful in managing your own investments and career or business.

You asked a profound question. You wanted to know the root cause of America's economic problems. "What's at the bottom of it all?" you wondered.

You are correct in assuming economics isn't the final answer. There is something even more fundamental than that—it's **law**.

In my next letter I'll begin telling you the story about the connection between our economic problems and our legal problems.

---

[3] Uncle Eric is referring to WHATEVER HAPPENED TO PENNY CANDY? by Richard J. Maybury, published by Bluestocking Press, web site: www.BluestockingPress.com; Phone: 800-959-8586.

This may sound hopelessly complex but, like most subjects, it's really quite simple once you understand it. Some years ago I read a book that brought Einstein's theory of relativity down to an eighth grade level. This convinced me that any subject can be made easy.

In other words, always beware of anyone who tells you a topic is above you or better left to experts. This person may, for some reason, be trying to shut you out. You *can* understand almost anything. If you know you are giving it your best effort and you are still finding an explanation difficult to grasp, it may be because the expert has poor communication skills. It could also be that the expert doesn't want you to grasp it. Many people are twice as smart as they think they are, but they've been intimidated into believing some topics are above them.

In my previous letters I mentioned one of my favorite remarks by Alexander Hamilton:

> Men give me some credit for genius. All the genius I have lies in this: When I have a subject in hand, I study it profoundly. Day and night it is before me. I explore it in all its bearings. My mind becomes pervaded with it. Then the effort which I make, the people are pleased to call the fruit of genius. It is the fruit of labor and thought.

I also like Thomas Edison's remark: "Genius is one percent inspiration and ninety-nine percent perspiration."

Before we get started I should add a few other notes of caution.

First, this will not be an objective, unbiased presentation. I believe America's Founders were right about law, **power**, and government. Through my letters and their own words, I think you, too, will draw some rather startling conclusions — conclusions that might not be consistent with what you've already been taught. Throughout your life you've only heard one side of the story. I believe you are old enough now to hear the other. You are asking good, honest questions, and they deserve good, honest answers.

Second, in a few places I'll mention religion. Please don't be alarmed. What I have to say won't contradict any of your religious principles. Come to think of it, nothing I have to say will conflict with the principles of any other religion, either. Religion is part of American history. **Legislation** has erased it from your history books. To study law without including religious history is to hear only one side of the story. You are ready for the other.

Please keep an open mind. I'm confident you'll soon be entirely comfortable, and even excited, about these ideas. America's Founders were so captivated by them they were willing to risk their lives for them.

> *"It may be affirmed, on the best grounds, that no small share of the present embarrassments of America is to be charged on the blunders of our governments. ... What indeed are all the repealing, explaining, and amending laws, which fill and disgrace our voluminous codes, but so many monuments of deficient wisdom."*
> — *James Madison*
> *Federalist #62*

> *"The facility and excess of lawmaking seem to be the diseases to which our governments are most liable."*
> — *James Madison*
> *Federalist #62*

If you are like most of the people to whom I've introduced these ideas, your mind will quickly flood with challenges and questions. "But what about this? What about that?" Be patient, we'll cover all important points, and I'll do my best to answer all your questions. The bridge to the Promised Land was torn down years ago and we must rebuild it one brick at a time before we can cross over.

In places I will be critical of **politics**. Please don't get the impression I'm being unpatriotic. The **government** is not the **country**. I've been around the world and visited many lands, from highly advanced Switzerland to horribly backward India, and would not want to live anywhere but here.

America is special and everyone knows it. I remember an elderly innkeeper in a picturesque little village in the Austrian Alps, a prosperous place. He asked where I was from and I said America. With a wistful look in his eyes he exclaimed, "Ah, a dream, a dream!"

In 1785, Thomas Jefferson went to Europe. He wrote back to James Monroe:

> My God! how little do my countrymen know what precious blessings they are in possession of and which no other people on earth enjoy. I confess I had no idea of it myself. While we shall see multiplied instances of Europeans going to live in America, I will venture to say, no man now living will ever see an instance of an American removing to settle in Europe, and continuing there.

The fact that I care so much about this wonderful country is one major reason I write these letters. Again, you deserve to hear the other side of the story about democracy, power, and government.

For now, remember that a **nation's** economic system is a result of its legal system. Or, economics is just a symptom, the cause is law.

Uncle Eric

"My God! how little do my countrymen know what precious blessings they are in possession of and which no other people on earth enjoy."
                                        — Thomas Jefferson

2

A Higher Authority

Dear Chris,

Much of what we will be covering in these letters will be foreign to you because it's been almost completely erased from American culture. You could ask your parents or teachers but odds are that they couldn't help you much. Most of this will be as new to them as it is to you.

But this is also what will make it fun. You'll be exploring a world few living Americans have ever seen; they don't even know it exists. When we're through, you'll be amazed at how much more you understand of daily life and important public issues than your friends do. So let's get started.

America was founded foremost on the belief that there is a **Higher Authority** than any human authority and a **Higher Law** than any human law.

Different creeds use different names when discussing this Higher Authority.

Thomas Jefferson and other American Founders often referred to Nature, but most just said God. The first paragraph of the Declaration of Independence contained an artful combination: ". . . the Laws of Nature and of Nature's God. . ."

George Washington seemed to believe in a personal, Biblical God that cared about humans as individuals. He was often seen on his knees praying.

Thomas Paine believed in a less personal "Nature" that was systematic, almost mechanical. Paine was convinced laws of morality could be discovered through scientific observation and logic. He wrote a wonderful book about this, called THE AGE OF REASON, and agreed with Greek philosopher Plutarch who said, "To follow God and obey reason is the same thing." Thomas Jefferson leaned this way, too.

Incidentally, Paine isn't well known today, but if we count Jefferson as the most important of the Founders, Paine was probably number two. His writing rallied Americans to the cause, and his pamphlet COMMON SENSE led to the Declaration of Independence.

In the American tradition, what counts is that we assume there is a Higher Authority than any human authority and a Higher Law than any human law.

In a speech before the Heritage Foundation, U.S. Supreme Court Judge Clarence Thomas quoted John Quincy Adams as saying:

Our political way of life is by the laws of nature, of nature's God, and of course presupposes the existence of God, the **moral** ruler of the universe, and a rule of right and wrong, of just and unjust, binding upon man, preceding all institutions of human society and of government.

The last nine words of that statement are the most important.

The major religions and philosophies all teach the existence of a Higher Authority. One of the most dramatic stories is in the Muslim Koran.

The Koranic story says Pharaoh was shown Allah's "mightiest miracle, but he denied it and rebelled." The Pharaoh "quickly went away and, summoning all his men, made to them a proclamation. 'I am your supreme Lord,' he said." The Koran then tells us Allah "smote him," and goes on to warn, "Surely in this there is a lesson for the God-fearing."

Says the Bible, "No man can serve two masters." The first of the Ten Commandments taught by Jews and Christians is, "I am the Lord thy God, thou shalt not have strange gods before me."

The Koran's story about the Pharaoh says it one way and the First Commandment says it another, but it's the same message. As far as I know, every major religion has something to say about a Higher Authority, but few these days say it very loudly.

Chris, how do you feel about what we've covered so far? To me it seems only logical. Imagine if there were no authority higher than the government. Governments are, after all, nothing more than collections of exceedingly human politicians and bureaucrats. What if these people who are mere flesh and blood like you and me were the top, the be all and end all, the final answer? How depressing. And frightening.

It's time I introduce you to the idea of a Higher Law.

Uncle Eric

3

A Higher Law

Dear Chris,

As mentioned in the previous remark by John Quincy Adams, America's Founders assumed the Higher Authority has given us a Higher Law that we must all learn and obey. In his excellent book THE AMERICAN TRADITION, historian Clarence B. Carson quotes Alexander Hamilton:

> Good and wise men, in all ages, have...supposed that the Deity... has constituted an eternal and immutable law, which is indispensably obligatory upon all mankind, prior to any human institution whatever.

Notice Hamilton said obligatory upon all mankind. No exceptions. This is very important. Higher Law applies to everyone equally.

This is what is meant by those five words in the Declaration of Independence "all men are created equal." No one gets any special privileges or exemptions from the Law. If something is prohibited for you and me, it's prohibited for kings, dukes, presidents, minorities, majorities, and everyone else.

Majorities? Thomas Jefferson said:

It is strangely absurd to suppose that a million human beings collected together are not under the same moral laws which bind each of them separately.

The commandment does not say, "Thou shalt not steal unless the majority votes for it." Nor does it say, "Thou shalt not steal unless you believe it is necessary." It says only, "Thou shalt not steal." Period. No exceptions.

I'm sure your parents have taught you that an American bows to no one. Americans stand tall, they look each other straight in the eye and they shake hands. This may sound like a small thing but it's profoundly important. Each time it happens it is a reconfirmation that no one is exempt from the law, all are equal. Equal rights, equal responsibilities. To bow is to open the door to exceptions.

Incidentally, this belief in a Higher Authority and a Higher Law goes back thousands of years. In the book ANCIENT LAW published in 1861, legal historian Henry Sumner Maine pointed out that in researching early political and legal organizations, "symptoms of this belief meet us on all sides." Maine refers to a "supernatural presidency" assumed by most original legal systems.

But already I can hear you asking, "If the Higher Authority has given us a Higher Law, how do we know what this Law is?"

Good question. After all, religions and philosophies often disagree. Is there a common ground where they all meet?

Yes, most emphatically, yes. In my next letter I'll begin the story about the world's best system for learning and applying Higher Law.

By the way, most of the Founders' work has been forgotten. I doubt one American in a thousand ever reads it any more.

Ask your friends. I'll bet they know little more than that George Washington chopped down a cherry tree and Ben Franklin flew a kite.

These were some of the wisest men in all human history. Their words, and warnings, are filled with insight. A half hour with Thomas Jefferson is more enlightening than a week with anyone else I know, except maybe James Madison or Patrick Henry. You'll be amazed at how much farther you can see when you are standing on the shoulders of Jefferson.

However, the Founders weren't perfect. Thomas Paine was fond of alcohol. Ben Franklin was a philanderer. Washington and Jefferson both owned slaves. Washington's pride led him into unforgivable military blunders.

These people were as human as you and me, and like you and me they were products of their times. But they believed a better world was possible and they rose above their origins to achieve it. This is what made them heroes. The liberty and abundance Americans enjoy today are mostly a result of the Founders' vision and efforts—and risks. They laid their lives on the line.

Explore their work, it's great.

Let me caution you to start not with books *about* the Founders but with their own work in their own words. Many books about American history — I'm tempted to say most now — are written by **socialists** who subtly discredit or trivialize the Founders and their principles. It's okay to read these books once you know enough about economics to spot the slant, but for now stick with the actual thoughts of the Founders themselves. One of the best sources: THE REVOLUTIONARY YEARS edited by Mortimer J. Adler.

Of course, in honesty I must admit that my own letters are slanted. I believe the Founders were right and I'm trying to convince you. As I said earlier, all your life you've heard only one side of the story and this is one of the few chances you'll have to hear the other.

Were all the American Founders squeaky clean in their motives? Certainly not. Madison was probably as close to being totally honorable as any human has ever been, but other Founders did have hidden agendas that included attempts to acquire power or money. Some undoubtedly tried to rig the Constitution to their own benefit. But, for reasons that remain unexplained to this day, the end result of all these competing interests was a Constitution of checks and balances that produced the most free and prosperous nation in all human history.

Before leaving the topic of religion I should mention this. You've probably met persons who hate other people's religions and accuse these others of being in league with the devil. Some even accuse others of being inherently warlike.

Any religion can be used for evil purposes, and many have at one time or another. The Crusades, the Inquisition, the Thirty Years War—history is filled with examples.

In these letters I will try to set ancient hatreds and rivalries aside and look only for what is best in each religion. I think you'll be delighted to find that the points where the religions are finest are also the points where they agree.

Chris, until my next letter remember that America was founded on the belief that a Higher Authority has given us a Higher Law which, in Hamilton's words, "is indispensably obligatory upon all mankind." Or, as Jefferson wrote, "All men are created equal."

Uncle Eric

4

Two Kinds Of Law

Dear Chris,

Throughout history, humans have used two basic kinds of legal systems. One is scientific and the other political.

Americans are no longer taught anything about these two kinds of law. Lawyers are aware of the two kinds but after they leave law school they are forced to work almost entirely in the political legal system. Never having much contact with scientific law, they soon forget it, and rarely mention it.

Many of America's Founders in 1776 and 1787 were **lawyers**. (At that time, lawyers were highly respected. Today, they are viewed with suspicion. Why the change? I'll talk about that in a future letter.)   America's Founders took care to insure that their new country would be founded on the principles of **scientific law**.

> *"In a democracy, opinions that upset everyone are sometimes exactly what we need. We should be teaching our children the scientific method and the Bill of Rights."*
>
> *— Carl Sagan & Ann Druyan[4]*

---

[4] "Real Patriots Ask Questions," PARADE MAGAZINE, Sept. 8, 1991.

To understand the differences between a political legal system and a scientific one, we must know how scientific law developed. We need to start all the way back in the Dark Ages around 500 A.D. My next few letters will be devoted entirely to scientific law, then we'll get into political law. When you've finished with my letters, you'll be ready to read THE ENTERPRISE OF LAW by Bruce L. Benson. This is a scholarly, thoroughly researched history of early common law systems and a plan for returning to them. But, let's begin here....

Fifteen centuries ago the Roman Empire collapsed. Barbarians had overrun Europe and set up **feudal** governments. These governments were bloodthirsty and brutal but, for the common people, they had one good point, they were lazy. They had little interest in the day-to-day affairs of the people. As long as the commoners paid taxes and fought in whatever wars they were ordered to fight in, their new governments left them alone.

This meant many kingdoms had no government court systems. When two individuals had a dispute, they were left to work it out on their own.

We can imagine what happened. Disputes often led to brawls or worse. After several bloody incidents, the commoners would surely begin looking for ways to avoid violence.

It's likely that when two individuals had a dispute, their families and friends would gather round and tell them to find some neutral third party to listen to their stories and make a decision.

Legal historians tell us the most highly respected and neutral third party in the community was usually a clergyman. The opponents would be brought before this clergyman and he would listen to both sides of their story.

The clergyman would consult moral guidelines such as the Ten Commandments and make a decision. The grapevine would spread this decision throughout the community. It would become a **precedent** for later decisions. Precedent is very important.

The reasoning behind it was simple. The fundamental nature of homo sapiens doesn't change much; what was right yesterday remains right today. Notice the emphasis on basics, on eternal truths.

Humans seem to have a built-in desire for legal systems based on precedent. What parent hasn't heard, "If Johnny can do it why can't I?" Each family has its own body of law developed one **case** at a time.

This law can be complex. Every child knows that the specific definitions of such phrases as "on time" and "too late" can be very important. Loopholes are sought like gold nuggets. The parents are under continual pressure to hone their rulings so that no misunderstandings are possible.

This method of evolving law on a case by case basis is called **case law**. Developed by judges, it was the beginning of scientific law. In a future letter I'll explain what made it scientific.

As decades passed, the precedents were written down and kept in a safe place. Persons who were not too clear about how to handle an unusual business transaction or some other sticky matter could study them to better plan ahead and avoid problems.

Eventually some of the clergymen became so skilled at listening to cases and making sound judgments that they acquired much prestige. Demand for their services grew and they became full-time **judges**. The body of precedents they produced became the law of common usage, the "**common law**."

A key point: Common law was based on religious and philosophical principles. This is how it determined right and wrong. What other way is there?

In 1897, Supreme Court Justice Oliver Wendell Holmes, Jr. pointed out, "The law is full of phraseology drawn from morals."[5]

Chris, in my next letter I will continue talking about scientific law. Specifically I will introduce you to the two fundamental principles underlying the old common law. After a half-dozen or so letters we'll get into **political law**, then government.

Until next time, remember two points: First, there are two kinds of law, political and scientific. Second, the old common law was a scientific legal system that grew out of court decisions — precedents — based on religious principles. In its early years common law had little connection with government, it was spawned by the religions.

Uncle Eric

---

[5] See the article "The Path of the Law" by Oliver Wendell Holmes, Jr., from the book, LAW, edited by Sara Robbins, Macmillan Publishing, New York, 1990, p. 276.

5

The Two Fundamental Laws

Dear Chris,

A major problem a common law judge encountered was disputes between persons from different communities or of different religions. Guidelines on which cases were decided had to be those which all reasonable persons held in common.

After much thought, the judges came up with **two fundamental laws** on which all major religions and philosophies agree: (1) do all you have agreed to do, and (2) do not **encroach** on other persons or their property. A simple formula, 17 words. BLACK'S LAW DICTIONARY defines encroach as follows:

> To enter by gradual steps or stealth into the possessions or rights of another; to trespass or intrude. To gain or intrude unlawfully upon the lands, property, or authority of another.

Each religion or philosophy expresses these laws in different ways but all concur on these two laws—and not much else.

The not much else is as important as the two laws. I'll explain shortly.

About the law of **agreements**, the Bible says, "Better it is that thou shouldest not vow, than that thou shouldest vow and not pay."[6]

The Koran says, "Woe unto the unjust who, when others measure for them, exact in full, but when they measure or weigh for others, defraud them."[7]

About encroaching on others or their property, Judaism and Christianity both say, "Thou shalt not steal" and "Thou shalt not murder."

It's amazing how close the wording can sometimes be. In Christianity, Jesus says, "Do unto others what you would want others to do unto you." One of Judaism's great teachers, Hillel, says, "Do not do unto others what you do not want others to do unto you."

The same thought, do unto others, is contained in the Confucian philosophy.[8] This originated in China four centuries ago and five-thousand miles apart from Christian and Jewish philosophies.

The two laws are stated and restated throughout the lore of all the great religions. They are the point on which all come together.

But only these two. Except for them we have little or no agreement about right and wrong.

> *"Can the liberties of a nation be thought secure when we have removed their only firm basis, a conviction in the minds of the people that these liberties are of the gift of God? That they are not to be violated but with his wrath?"*
>
> *— Thomas Jefferson*

---

[6] ECCLESIASTES, V, 1

[7] THE UNJUST, 83:1

[8] FREEDOM AND THE LAW by Bruno Leoni, Nash Publishing, Los Angeles, 1972, p. 14

So, these are the only two rules that can be enforced on everyone. To go beyond them would be encroachment.

Since encroachment is forbidden, each person is free to obey other laws if he or she wishes. If, for instance, you wish to obey laws requiring charity, compassion, respect, or something else, no one can rightfully interfere as long as you do not violate the two fundamental laws.

Common law was the body of definitions and procedures growing out of these two laws. "Do all you have agreed to do" was the basis of the part of common law called **contract law**.

"Do not encroach on other persons or their property" was the basis of **criminal law** and **tort law**. (Tort law concerns harm done by one person to another.)

This is how common law became the source of all our basic laws against theft, fraud, kidnapping, rape, murder, and so forth. A judge would listen to a case and find that someone had broken an agreement or encroached.

Did you think these acts were made illegal by Congress? No, they were illegal long before Congress existed. Long before Columbus discovered America, they were found to be illegal by judges in precedents based on religious principles.

Why are Americans no longer taught anything about common law? Hard to say. My guess is that since tax-supported schools are prohibited from teaching anyone's religion (and rightly so, whose religion would they teach?) these schools are unable to teach about the origin of our most important laws. As a result, few Americans grow up today knowing anything about common law. You can test this yourself. Ask any adult, what was common law?

Unable to teach about common law, the schools teach only political law.

Many religions teach the basics of common law without even realizing that common law grew from these rules.

Church attendance is declining. Reliable statistics on the number of Americans who attended church regularly in the early 1800s are hard to come by, but I don't think any historian would disagree that it was a large number, 75 percent or more. By 1990 it was down to 40 percent.[9] Many clergy are distressed at the decline in their congregations.

This distresses me, too, because I suspect this is causing a serious problem for parents. The religions were the source of the idea of **Natural Law**[10]—meaning the laws of the universe that common law judges were trying to discover. Americans absorbed this idea automatically through their religious training. I am afraid that many who throw out religion are also unknowingly throwing out Natural Law. They are left with the inescapable conclusion that right and wrong are only matters of opinion. They no longer know what to teach their children. Rather than using objective truth, Higher Law, they resort to subjective opinion. The result will be a generation, not of **immoral** children, but of **amoral** children.

In its early years, common law was a private legal system completely independent of government. This is important. Many Americans today believe law and government are nearly the same thing, but this is incorrect. Law and government are two very different institutions and they do not necessarily go together.[11] Law is a service provided by courts, and a code of conduct. Government is something much

---

[9] "Still Praying," THE ECONOMIST, May 20, 1989, p. 35.

[10] The fact that a political group may have the words "natural law" in its name does not mean it necessarily has any interest in the type of Natural Law explained in this book. One test is to check the party platform to see if they want to protect your rights to your property.

[11] Nor are the government and the country the same thing. When we pledge allegiance to the flag, exactly what are we pledging allegiance to? Our homeland? Our government?

different. Law came from religious principles, government came from...what?

We'll get into that in a future letter. First we have more ground to cover about common law and political law. In my next letter I'll explain how common law was enforced.

Incidentally, you might be wondering if many people today agree on the two fundamental laws. For years I have been writing articles and traveling around the U.S. giving speeches about these laws. I've delivered the message to hundreds of thousands and have never had anyone disagree with these two laws. Not one person.

Some members of an audience will disagree with almost anything. I even had one person tell me he didn't like my tie — but not these two laws.

If you meet people who disagree with these laws, ask if they'd like to live in a world where these laws are not obeyed.

Some people do disagree with the idea of a Higher Authority. They believe there is nothing higher than the government. But they still agree with the two laws. They just believe the government is entitled to disobey these laws whenever officials believe this is necessary. These persons say the rest of us must obey, but government officials are special.

Until my next letter remember there are two fundamental laws on which all major religions and philosophies agree: 1) do all you have agreed to do, and 2) do not encroach on other persons or their property. These rules are the basis of common law, which held that everyone must obey — no exceptions. All men are created equal.

Incidentally, always bear in mind that an agreement must be voluntary. An agreement resulting from force or deception is not binding.

Chris, let me finish with a very important point. Except when I say otherwise, I will always be writing about these laws as they apply to competent adults, not children or persons with mental impairments.

No one has ever found a completely logical system for dealing with children or the mentally impaired. All agree that rights and responsibilities are attached to mental ability, but none agree on which rights, or which responsibilities, or what level of mental ability.

If a three-year old stole something, no court would do much about it. If a twenty-one-year old steals, any court would. But where do we draw the line, and why there? No one has ever figured this out—the lines are drawn arbitrarily.[12]

Again, in these letters, except where I specifically say something about children, we are talking about adults only.

Uncle Eric

The Two Laws

Do all you have agreed to do.

Do not encroach on other persons or their property.

---

[12] For a partial solution to the problem of children's rights, see the *Agreement Between Parent and Child* and *Agreement Between Teacher and Student* in the appendix.

6

Enforcement of Early Common Law

Dear Chris,

Now that you know a bit about the early common law you may be asking how this law was enforced. If early common law had no connection with government, then a judge could not use police, troops, or prisons to enforce decisions. Could a criminal simply walk away?

The short answer is yes. The longer answer is yes, but...

Suppose one person harmed another. The judge would instruct the offender to make **restitution** to the victim. If the offender refused, the judge could then use a procedure called **outlawry**.

Under outlawry the judge was saying to the perpetrator, "We will not force the law onto you. You have decided to be outside the law, so be it. And, since you do not accept the responsibilities of the law, neither shall you have its protections. From now on your legal status shall be no different from that of a rabbit or any other wild animal outside the law."

The description of this person who had decided to be an outlaw would be publicized. Then anyone — let me emphasize, anyone — could hunt him down and enslave him, kill him or, perhaps, cook and eat him like a rabbit. It was none of the court's business, the outlaw had made his choice. The victim might even hire a bounty hunter to track the criminal down and sell him as a beast of burden.

It's difficult to believe there were many cases in which judges found it necessary to use outlawry.

The word outlaw is from the common law principle of outlawry.

Of course there was always the possibility someone would make a mistake. The bounty hunter might capture the wrong person. The police sometimes do this today. But under common law the bounty hunter had a mighty incentive to do the job right. If he harmed an innocent person he could end up an outlaw himself.

Courts could make mistakes, too. So, there was an **appeal** system that enabled persons who disagreed with decisions to tell their story to a higher court.

You may also be interested in the system of restitution. Today when a person harms someone, courts assume he owes a debt to society. He goes to prison where he makes license plates for the state. Everyone, including the victim, pays additional taxes to support him.

Under common law the offender's debt was to his victim. His obligation was to restore his victim as nearly as possible to the victim's original condition. This included paying the victim for all damages including time lost from work, court expenses, emotional stress, you name it. A criminal who harmed someone seriously could end up the victim's slave, and the victim could rent him to other individuals or companies.

In the case of an outlaw, the victim could even kill the slave, but this probably didn't happen often. A criminal-slave was worth a lot of money. The victim would be more likely to sell him rather than do anything that would damage him or otherwise reduce his value.

Many cultures evolved common law systems. This seems to be a natural tendency for humans. Early on, several of these systems came up with detailed lists of prices for doing harm.

Clovis, founder of the Frankish kingdom, had a group of lawyers write down the *Lex Salica (Law of the Salian Franks)* around 508 A.D. This contained a list of **wergild**, or restitutions. In a study called BIRTH OF FRANCE, historian Katharine Scherman wrote that in the *Lex Salica*, "The criminal's first liability was to the victim."

Restitutions were split 50-50 between the victim (or in the case of murder, the victim's family) and the government that had apprehended him. Prices were denominated in the bezant gold coin which contained 65 grains of gold and was equal to about a month's wages.[13]

For the murder of an adult male, the wergild was 200 bezants. For the murder of a pregnant woman, 700.

Under the category of assault and battery there was a list of prices for injuring a finger, an ear, and other body parts. For putting out an eye the wergild was 100 bezants.

---

[13] Using values derived from wage rates of the late Roman Empire given by Robert L. Schuettinger and Eamonn F. Butler in the 1979 edition of FORTY CENTURIES OF WAGE AND PRICE CONTROLS, p. 24.

Lesser offenses were covered in detail, too. For stroking a woman's hand against her will, 15 bezants; for touching her bosom, 35; for rape, 62.5.

But the *Lex Salica* said nothing about making license plates for the state.

Historian Scherman says imprisonment in those days was rare, as it was under most common law systems. A person who sits rotting in a jail cell can't earn money to pay the debts he owes his victims. And his victims certainly don't want to pay higher taxes to support him.

Chris, if you'd like to convert these prices to modern equivalents, the average wage in the U.S. at the beginning of the 21st century was about $2700 per month; so, the equivalent cost of stroking a woman's hand against her will would be $40,500.

Before we leave the subject of outlawry and restitution, notice how advanced these systems were. When damage was done, the person who did it was responsible for fixing it. This was fifteen centuries ago during the Dark Ages. What does this tell you about our legal systems today? Think about it.

I recommend a book called EARLY CHRISTIAN IRELAND: INTRODUCTION TO THE SOURCES by Kathleen Hughes (Cornell University Press, 1972). Historian Hughes gives a fine description of the insurance organizations the early Irish used for enforcement of their common law and for taking care of victims. By today's standards this system was wonderfully sophisticated and effective. It was in full operation in 600 A.D.

In my next letter we'll talk about common law's scientific nature. Until then, remember that the ultimate enforcement system for the early common law was outlawry, and the offender's first responsibility was to his victim.

Uncle Eric

7

How Do We Know If It's Law?

Dear Chris,

The primary source of common law was custom. Through trial and error in their relationships, people learned the rules that worked, and these rules became law. To prevent trivial whim and opinion from becoming law, courts had guidelines for deciding if a custom should be law.

> Blackstone provided in his COMMENTARIES a clear account of tests which customs should meet before they were admitted to have the force of law. ... Good custom is: (1) *ancient,* no man can remember the beginning of it, (2) *continuous,* the rights claimed under it have never been abandoned or interrupted, (3) *peaceable,* supported by the common consent of those using the custom, (4) *reasonable,* in the light of 'legal' reason, (5) *certain,* in the sense of being ascertainable, (6) *compulsory,* it is not left to the opinion of every man whether he will obey or not, (7) *consistent,* for one custom cannot contradict another custom without producing an absurdity.
>
> — ORIGINS OF THE COMMON LAW
> by Arthur R. Hogue

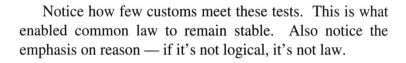

Notice how few customs meet these tests. This is what enabled common law to remain stable. Also notice the emphasis on reason — if it's not logical, it's not law.

Uncle Eric

8

Logic and Atoms

Dear Chris,

Many years ago there was a mathematician who was interested in physics. With the assistance of his colleagues, he discovered that all matter is composed of tiny, invisible particles which he called atoms. His work led him to the conclusion that atoms differ from one another in form and position, are constantly in motion, and are arranged in groups which are now called molecules.

None of this mathematician's discoveries are surprising to us today, we are all familiar with the basics of nuclear physics. What is surprising is that the mathematician was Democritus and he was a citizen of Greece in 400 B.C. He made all his discoveries about the atom without the aid of cyclotrons, nuclear reactors, electron microscopes, or other high-tech equipment. The only tool he used was his brain, he used **logic**.

In the past, most judges were similar in thinking to Democritus. They believed it was possible to discover the laws of the universe through logic. And they differed from Democritus only in that they were trying to discover not the laws of physics, but the **laws of morality**.

The common law judges were very aware that law can involve **force**. The judges were trying to discover the principles which would guide them in the use of force. They wanted the force to be applied only sparingly and only against persons who had harmed someone.

American Founder Thomas Paine wrote, "Man cannot make principles, he can only discover them." This is crucially important. It explains exactly the premise of both **science** and the common law.

Under common law, the judge was a sort of combination philosopher and scientist. His task was to discover the principles that make civilization possible — principles such as "Thou shalt not steal" and "Thou shalt not murder" — and apply them in cases brought before him. He was a thinker in the tradition of Democritus, Newton, Galileo, and the other philosopher-scientists who were trying to discover how the universe works.

This is a major reason lawyers and judges were so highly respected. They had the status of scientists. It was their life's work to discover and apply correct moral principles. Some people today see lawyers as immoral, or at best, amoral.

A highly skilled common law judge would try to make all his decisions logically consistent with the two fundamental laws — do all you have agreed to do, and do not encroach on other persons or their property. Any law or decision that was not logically consistent with these laws was considered nonsense and was not binding.

This too is important. If it wasn't logical, it wasn't law.

One of the greatest lawyers in history once made the surprising revelation that EUCLID'S GEOMETRY was one of his most important law books. He studied it to be sure the logic of his cases was airtight. His name was Abraham Lincoln.

The merits of Lincoln's presidency are a subject of much debate. His war cost 600,000 American lives, more even than the Second World War.

But Lincoln's career as a lawyer was undeniably stellar, and this was largely because of his careful attention to logic.

One of the most important characteristics of common law was its certainty. It had evolved very carefully over many centuries, changing little from one decade to the next. The two fundamental laws remained always in place, a stabilizing force. Investors and business people could expect their economic environment to remain reasonably orderly.

In fact, common law was so logical and sensible that the typical American studied it and understood it! It was regarded as a source of wisdom. In his Pulitzer Prize winning book THE IDEOLOGICAL ORIGINS OF THE AMERICAN REVOLUTION, historian Bernard Bailyn writes,

> To the colonists it was a repository of experience in human dealings embodying the principles of **justice**, equity, and rights; above all it was a form of history — ancient, indeed immemorial, history; constitutional and national history; and, as history, it helped explain the movement of events and the meaning of the present.

The great British statesman Edmund Burke said of early America, "In no country, perhaps, in the world, is law so general a study." He observed that "all who read, and most do read, endeavor to obtain some smattering in that science. I have been told by an eminent bookseller, that in no branch of his business ... were so many books as those on law exported to the colonies."

Notice Burke referred to law as a science. This was a widespread attitude. Charles Warren was assistant attorney general to the U.S. in 1914-18. In describing Harvard's early law curriculum, he called law a science.

Here's an interesting point. A present-day myth says the early Americans were illiterate bumpkins who, because they had no schooling, had no education. Far from it. British general Thomas Gage was trying to govern Massachusetts in 1774-75 when he complained that Americans were impossible to buffalo, they were all lawyers.[14]

How many Americans today can read well enough to handle law books?

Have you ever read Thomas Paine's COMMON SENSE? In THE FREEMAN magazine, journalist J. Brian Phillips writes,

> COMMON SENSE had an unprecedented **influence** on the minds of the American people. Paine estimated that 150,000 copies were sold in the first year; other estimates went as high as 500,000 copies. With fewer than three million people in the colonies at the time, either figure is astounding. Nearly every adult read the pamphlet.

By today's standards COMMON SENSE is heavy reading, college level. These people had to have been well educated, at least by today's standards.

Chris, self-teaching is a form of education that sticks, and it can continue and remain enjoyable for life. I hope you'll follow the example of these early Americans. It's probably the only way you'll learn much about common law.

---

[14] LAW IN AMERICA by Bernard Schwartz, McGraw-Hill, NY 1974, p. 3.

In a future letter we will delve more deeply into the scientific nature of common law. Until then, remember that under the old common law, if it's not logical, it's not law.

By the way, I've noticed that this logic in the old common law is what causes many lawyers to become hooked on law. When they first encounter it in law school they are struck by its wondrous beauty. They know — they feel deep in their hearts — that they are in the presence of something profound. It's much the same feeling doctors experience when they study the human body, or astronomers when they study the heavens. They sense they are making contact with...what? Too bad common law is gone.

Uncle Eric

Thomas Paine

Engraved by
Illman & Sons
after a painting by
George Romney.
Reproduced from the
DICTIONARY OF
AMERICAN PORTRAITS,
published by Dover
Publications, Inc., in
1967

"...one thing you have to say about science: It delivers the goods. If you want to know when the next eclipse of the Sun will be, you might try magicians and mystics, but you'll do much better with scientists. They can tell you within a fraction of a second when an eclipse will happen decades or centuries in the future, how long it'll last and where on Earth you should be standing to get a good look. If you want to know the sex of your unborn child, you can consult astrologers or plumb-bob danglers all you want, but they'll be right, on average, only one time in two. If you want real accuracy, try science.

"What is the secret of its success? Partly, it's this: There is a built-in error-correcting machinery. There are no forbidden questions in science, no matters too sensitive or delicate to be probed, no sacred truths. There is an openness to new ideas combined with the most rigorous, skeptical scrutiny of all ideas, a sifting of the wheat from the chaff. Arguments from authority are worthless. It makes no difference how smart, august or beloved you are. You must prove your case in the face of determined, expert criticism. Diversity and debate between contending views are valued."

— Carl Sagan and Ann Druyan
"Real Patriots Ask Questions"
PARADE MAGAZINE
September 8, 1991

9
Ambient Encroachment
& Tacit Contracts

"Only a virtuous people are capable of freedom. As nations become corrupt and vicious, they have more need of masters."
— *Benjamin Franklin*

Dear Chris,

In this letter I'll try to clear up two points that can lead to confusion. The first concerns something we might call **ambient** encroachment, meaning the surrounding level of encroachment.

Most communities permit a small amount of encroachment. This is an amount widely accepted as tolerable or necessary.

You can phone someone between the hours of, say, 9AM and 9PM, or you can stroll up their front walk and knock on their door. But don't phone them at 3AM or tramp through their flower beds. If you exceed the ambient level of encroachment, you'll owe them for the inconvenience or damage you've caused.

Some individuals permit more encroachment than others. One person may not mind if strangers knock on her back door. Another may want strangers to come only to her front door.

The safest course is to always err on the side of caution. If you must encroach, be as polite and unintrusive as possible.

Try to see it from the other person's point of view. Your own privacy, peace, and quiet are important to you, so don't disrupt someone else's. Do unto others...

Also, never touch another person or his property unless you are sure you have his permission. Give him space. He will trust you more and be more friendly and helpful as soon as he realizes you are trying not to encroach.

I've been around the world and in the company of all kinds of people, from scientists and jet pilots to the most primitive jungle Indians. This works everywhere.

The second point to clear up is that of unspoken **contracts**. An agreement does not need to be in writing to be binding. Most contracts are unspoken or **tacit**.

If you walk into a grocery store to buy a candy bar, numerous tacit contracts are in force. The first is from the fact that the door is open. By leaving the door open the owner is agreeing to allow you to come in as long as you don't do any harm. He hasn't said this to you directly, it's understood and it's **binding**.

The next contract concerns the candy. You are permitted to pick it up and examine it, but not damage it or move it to another location. The owner has not said this to you directly, but it's understood, or customary, and it's binding.

You decide to buy this candy and take it to the register. You lay it on the counter and the clerk rings it up. You give the money to the clerk, pick up the candy, and leave the store.

All this has happened without a word spoken, but a complex agreement has been executed, and it's binding. The store owner has guaranteed that the candy is what the wrapper says it is. It's sugar, not salt; almonds not peanuts; and, it won't poison you.

On your side of this tacit agreement, you are guaranteeing that the money you hand over is the type and amount the owner would reasonably expect. The quarters are genuine U.S. coins, not foreign coins, or slugs, or anything else of lesser value. (Why quarters for a candy bar today, when I paid a nickel when I was a kid? Do you remember the economics you learned through our prior letters?)[15]

Again, most contracts are unspoken, but they can be very complex, containing numerous guarantees you don't even think about. These guarantees are binding.

To have the best chance of getting the most for your money, get into the habit of asking yourself before every large purchase, "Exactly what am I agreeing to, and what is the other party agreeing to? What are we guaranteeing to each other?"

When dealing with friends, bear in mind that friends tend to give each other the benefit of the doubt when something goes wrong. They are less inclined to defend their interests than they are in cases where they are dealing with strangers. This can lead to hard feelings and shattered relationships because a friend can feel he is getting "the short end of the stick" if something goes wrong.

So, the more you care about a friend, the more careful you should be about clearly stating all parts of any agreement you have with him, especially parts that answer the question, "what if something goes wrong?" The best way to handle misunderstandings is to prevent them.

In making any agreement with a friend, you might want to follow the example of the old common law. Specify that if a dispute arises, you will choose a third party acceptable to you

---

[15] See WHATEVER HAPPENED TO PENNY CANDY? by Richard J. Maybury, published by Bluestocking Press, web site: www.BluestockingPress.com; Phone: 800-959-8586.

both. You will each tell your side of the story to this third party, and you each agree to abide by whatever decision the third party makes.

Another point. Your word should be your bond, and you should try to cultivate a reputation for this. It will be one of your most valuable pos-

> *"Neither the wisest constitution nor the wisest laws will secure the liberty and happiness of a people whose manners are universally corrupt."*
>
> — *Samuel Adams*

sessions and will open up opportunities that are not available to others who have reputations for being untrustworthy.

In other words, honesty can be profitable. People will pay extra to deal with someone they are sure is reliable. Do all you have agreed to do.

I will finish this letter by mentioning a survival tactic.

You've probably noticed that someone who encroaches in small ways may be inclined to encroach in large ways. Similarly, a person who will break agreements in small ways may be inclined to major **fraud**.

Before getting into any kind of close personal or business relationship, observe how the person behaves in minor situations. If he shows the slightest inclination to encroach or fudge on agreements, he may be a thug who will hurt you seriously if he thinks he can get away with it.

Try to develop an internal alarm. When you see someone break an agreement or encroach beyond the ambient level, your alarm should alert you: "Look out, someone who will do that might do anything."

The best people to deal with are those who are very reluctant to encroach and who are careful to always give all they have agreed to.

Uncle Eric

Fraud: An intentional perversion of truth for the purpose of inducing another in reliance upon it to part with some valuable thing belonging to him or to surrender a legal right. A false representation of a matter of fact, whether by words or by conduct, by false or misleading allegations, or by concealment of that which should have been disclosed, which deceives and is intended to deceive another so that he shall act upon it to his legal injury. Any kind of artifice employed by one person to deceive another.

— BLACK'S LAW DICTIONARY

Agreement: A concord of understanding and intention between two or more parties with respect to the effect upon their relative rights , or benefits, with the view of contracting an obligation, a mutual obligation.

— BLACK'S LAW DICTIONARY

Thomas Jefferson's
Maxims for the Conduct of a Young Man

1. Never spend your money before you have it.

2. Never buy what you don't want because it is cheap.   It will be dear[16] to you.

3. Pride costs more than hunger, thirst, and cold.

4. Never put off tomorrow what you can do today.

5. Never trouble another for what you can do yourself.

6. Think as you please and let others do so; you will then have no disputes.

7. How much pain have cost us the things which have never happened?

8. Take things away by their smooth handle.

9. When angry count to 10 before you speak.   If very angry 100.

10. When at table, remember that we never repent of having eaten or drunk too little.

---

[16] expensive

10

Economic Calculation

Dear Chris,

Do all you have agreed to do, and do not encroach on other persons or their property. These two fundamental laws have been more widely obeyed in America, by everyone, including government officials, than anywhere else. So, America became the most advanced nation ever seen on earth. Not until the 1970s did this advancement slow.

The reason these two fundamental laws create a progressive civilization with increasing abundance for all is something economists call **economic calculation**. It sounds complicated, but it's not. Here's how it works.

Suppose I offer to sell you something, say a pen, for five dollars. I will do so only if I want the five dollars more than the pen. You will agree to the trade only if you want the pen more than the five dollars.

In a **free trade**, both parties end up with something they value more than what they traded away. Otherwise they would not go to the trouble of trading.

Therefore, in a free trade, both parties profit. Both have their lives slightly improved.

> *"In transactions of trade it is not to be supposed that, as in gaming, what one party gains the other must necessarily lose. The gain to each may be equal. If A has more corn than he can consume, but wants cattle; and B has more cattle, but wants corn; exchange is gain to each; thereby the common stock of comforts in life is increased."*
>
> — Benjamin Franklin, 1706-1790 signer, Declaration of Independence

The sum of all the profits from all the free trades in a society is what we call progress. Free trade is the source of progress.

This is economic calculation in action. Humans produce and trade only when they think it will yield something they want more than the time, money, effort, and other factors required for the production and trade.

A key word here is think. Economic calculation is difficult, we sometimes make mistakes. Trades occasionally yield accidental losses. We have all had the experience of doing some kind of work or making a purchase that has us saying, "I wish I hadn't done that, it wasn't worth it."

Economic calculation is difficult and some transactions yield losses. But as long as both parties come to a transaction voluntarily, we know chances are good it will yield gains for both. Civilization will move slightly ahead.

Chris, I should point out here that this is a bit of an oversimplification. Not all profits bring advancement in the sense of being better off today than yesterday. Here's why.

Things break down and wear out. They get used up. Ask your parents about the cost of auto repairs and food, and you'll know what I'm talking about. Much profit goes toward just staying even, toward avoiding decline. So, only a portion of our profits goes toward genuine progress. We need a certain amount of profit just to keep from sliding back into the Dark Ages.

But to keep things simple, I'll continue speaking in terms of any profit being progress. Besides, it's true in a sense. Throughout history, most of mankind has lived in grinding poverty most of the time. If any of our ancestors had seen how we live now they'd have thought heaven on earth had been achieved. To them, merely staying where we are would be more than anyone could reasonably wish for.

Just bear in mind that when I speak of any profit being progress, I'm simplifying to make my explanations easier to grasp.

In my next letter we'll see what happens to economic calculation when someone violates the two fundamental laws. Until then, remember that free trade is the source of progress. In a free trade, both parties end up with something they value more than what they traded away. Otherwise they wouldn't go to the trouble of trading.

Uncle Eric

Do you know anyone old enough to remember the beforetime...

... when men walked on the moon? (As I write this, the last moon mission was launched in 1972.)

... when home ownership was a realistic possibility for most American families.

... when the typical middle-class family could get ahead with only one person working outside the home.

... when "real" wages (adjusted for inflation) rose continually.

... when the normal unemployment was only 3-4%.

... when poverty was declining.

... when good job opportunities were common.

... when stress was something engineers studied.

... when single-parent households were unusual.

... when most high-school students could read.

... when narcotic addiction was almost unknown.

... when you rarely saw a person who was home-
less or hungry.

... when you could leave your doors unlocked at
night.

... when it was automatically assumed that each
generation of Americans would eventually
live better than their parents.

"Recessions aside, the U.S. economy since about 1973 has been suffering from a slowly debilitating disease. Growth in productivity has dropped, the competitiveness of industry has declined, the once-steady rise in living standards has faltered, and wages have stagnated. Most Americans tell pollsters that they doubt their children's generation will live as well as they do. The American dream is fading."

— Alan Murray
"Outlook," WALL STREET JOURNAL
December 2, 1991

11

Force or Fraud

Dear Chris,

Suppose someone introduces force into the transaction. Suppose a third party — a government or a criminal, it does not matter — says you must purchase the pen even if it is not worth five dollars to you. If you don't, you will be punished.

We can expect this trade to still yield a profit for me because I participate voluntarily, but we cannot expect this for you. For you, the pen may be worth only four dollars, or it may be worth nothing at all. Perhaps you do not need it. So, the trade may cause you a loss.

When the two fundamental laws are not obeyed—when force or fraud enter a transaction—odds are that at least one party will suffer a loss. Someone will give up something he values more than what he receives in exchange. Civilization will move slightly backward.

In a government-controlled **economy**, force is involved in millions of transactions every day. Anything involving taxes involves force. So, millions of transactions yield losses every day. People are continually being forced to give up things they value more than what they get.

The presence of force is a near ironclad guarantee of loss. If losses were not happening, these people would go along voluntarily.

When the government grows large enough, the losses outnumber the gains and civilization moves backward. We apparently reached this point sometime in the early 1970s.

To summarize, scientific law permits effective economic calculation and progress. Political law...but that's another story we will cover in letters to come.

These are the essential facts of economic calculation. They tell us free markets are the source of America's legendary abundance, and they tell us why the two fundamental laws are necessary for an advancing civilization.

Chris, until my next letter, remember that in a free trade, chances are good that both parties will profit; civilization will move slightly ahead. But when force or fraud enters the transaction, chances are that one or both parties will suffer a loss; civilization will move backward. The loss may be well hidden but, given enough time, a good economist can spot it.

Uncle Eric

Chains of Agreements

In a free country we organize ourselves by chains of agreements. The farmer agrees to sell wheat to the mill. The miller agrees to sell flour to the bakery. The baker agrees to sell buns to the restaurant, and the restaurateur agrees to sell dinner to you and me.

Each person is a link in the chain, and all rely on each other. If any one person breaks his agreement, the chain fails, and all end up with less than they need.

12

The Lawless West

Dear Chris,

Persons who learn their history from Hollywood movies tend to believe the American West was a land overrun by lawless killers. It sometimes seems the gurus of Tinseltown have spent millions convincing us everything west of the Mississippi was gunfights and outlaws until U.S. marshals arrived.

The truth, of course, is much different and much too tame for a movie. Dodge City and a few other places were wild; but, by and large, the West was a peaceful place far less dangerous than most big cities today. It was LITTLE HOUSE ON THE PRAIRIE not GUNSMOKE.

Think about it. Why do we recognize the names Jesse James and Black Bart when we do not know the names of the criminals who roam the streets of our cities today? Because Jesse James and Black Bart were unusual. Today most cities contain hundreds of these thugs, and many are far more bloodthirsty than Jesse James or Black Bart were in their worst nightmares.

Life on a frontier is hard work. This is where we find not the worst but the finest specimens of mankind. Cities are where we find the parasites because cities are where the parasites find the most victims.

The common law tradition holds that there is no such thing as a lawless place. The law exists, just as the laws of physics and chemistry exist. Even if we choose not to learn or follow the law, it is still there producing its inevitable results. Obey the law and life gets better, disobey and life gets worse. It's automatic.

The pioneers believed this and lived accordingly. They were law-abiding despite the absence of police; it was ingrained in them.

This more than anything else is what was once meant by the word American. An American was a person with specific, definable principles. He had character, honor. He obeyed common law even when no police were nearby.

Looking outward at the rest of the world, the American saw barbarism, a barbarism caused by the absence of common law principles. The American had made a deliberate, conscious choice to be honorable and civilized. This is how he built the most advanced civilization ever known.

Between 1820 and 1940, 38 million people came to America, often risking their lives to do so. They wanted to live under these principles. This is why Americans have always been known as one of the most law-abiding peoples in the world. They chose to be.

In most nations, patriotism is a dedication to the **homeland**, the geographic area. America is different. With the possible exception of Switzerland, America was the first nation ever to be founded on a set of moral principles. Even today, America remains more of an idea than a place. That lump-in-the-throat patriotism inspired by the Liberty Bell or the Statue of Liberty comes as a result of what the country *means,* not where it is.

This also points to one of the most fascinating aspects of common law: it truly is scientifically provable. We can measure the results.

The nations in which the two fundamental laws are more widely obeyed by everyone, including government officials ("all men are created equal"), are those that have higher average incomes, less poverty, less crime, longer life spans, better health, more literacy, and so forth. By almost any gauge, these nations are better places to live.

See for yourself. Where would you rather live—the U.S. or Russia? Switzerland or Ethiopia? New Zealand or Iraq?

The early Americans understood this. They were immigrants who had fled poorer nations. To them, the superiority of common law principles was obvious. They had seen with their own eyes that the more political law a nation had, the greater the extremes of wealth and poverty, and the smaller the middle class.

Perhaps this gives you a hint of what I'll soon be writing in regard to political law.

Early Americans also saw immediate, everyday benefits of following the two fundamental laws. This was expressed in sayings such as, honesty is the best policy.

French writer and moralist Jean de la Bruyere explained, "A show of a certain amount of honesty is in any profession or business the surest way of growing rich." This is because buyers and employers seek honest people. They don't want to get ripped off.

In my opinion, in America today we place far too much emphasis on intelligence and too little on character. Intelligence is great, but only if used in honorable ways. I like George Washington's remark:

I hope I shall always possess firmness and virtue enough to maintain what I consider the most enviable of all titles, the character of an "Honest Man."

What do you think Washington would say about computer viruses? These are small programs designed to secretly spread from one computer to another and do damage. They can be written only by a brilliant intellect. Today hundreds of these viruses are harming millions of innocent people.

Virus creators are highly intelligent and highly barbaric. I cannot imagine anything more terrifying than that combination, and I'm afraid it is the wave of the future. If we don't find a way to stop it, it will destroy us, and soon. Please tell others about the two fundamental laws.

Until my next letter, remember, the two fundamental laws are one part of religion (the only part?) that is scientifically provable. Where these laws are more widely obeyed, life is better.

Uncle Eric

In most nations, patriotism is a dedication to the homeland, the geographic area. America is different. With the possible exception of Switzerland, America was the first nation ever to be founded on a set of moral principles. Even today, America remains more of an idea than a place. That lump-in-the-throat patriotism inspired by the Liberty Bell or the Statue of Liberty comes as a result of what the country means, not where it is.

The Results of the Two Fundamental Laws are Scientifically Measurable

	Nation	GDP per Capita	Male Life Expectancy	Telephones per person	Internet Users per household	TVs per household	Infant Deaths per 1000
Where the laws are most widely obeyed.	Australia	38,100	79.25	1.46	1.37	1.86	4.75
	Canada	39,100	78.69	1.19	2.26	1.91	5.04
	Switzerland	41,800	78.03	1.72	1.39	1.05	4.18
	USA	46,900	75.65	1.36	1.89	2.19	6.26
Where the laws are less widely obeyed.	Mexico	14,200	73.25	0.79	0.86	1.14	18.42
	Panama	11,700	74.47	0.86	0.64	0.79	12.67
	S. Africa	10,100	49.81	0.96	0.42	0.55	44.42
	S. Korea	27,600	75.45	1.39	2.13	1.06	4.26
Where the laws are least obeyed.	Ethiopia	800	52.92	0.02	0.02	0.03	80.80
	Pakistan	2,500	63.40	0.53	0.68	0.71	65.14
	Uganda	1,300	51.66	0.14	0.29	0.13	64.82
	Zaire (Dem. Republic of Congo)	300	52.58	0.10	0.02	0.01	81.21

Data Source: CIA FACTBOOK, 2009 WORLD ALMANAC, 2009 TIME (BRITANNICA) ALMANAC

GDP per Capita: Purchasing Power Parity (PPP)
Telephones = Land Lines plus Mobile Cellular (CIA Factbook)

Notice citizens in a higher category enjoy several times the wealth of those in the category immediately beneath them. The American and Swiss have nearly forty times the wealth of persons in the least free nations where poverty and starvation are frequent. In America and Switzerland, economic calculation is less effective than years ago, but it is still working to a large extent. In the least free nations it has been nearly destroyed. In these nations, force and fraud are everywhere, and the governments are the worst offenders. Notice South Korea's political reforms have been moving it upward, it's not far from category one.

13

Natural Rights

"The natural liberty of man is to be free from any superior power on Earth, and not to be under the will or legislative authority of man, but only to have the law of nature for his rule."
— *Samuel Adams, 1772*

Dear Chris,

This system of law we have been talking about is sometimes called **Natural Law**. The American Founders believed the moral laws that govern humans are a subset of the natural laws that govern the universe.

Where these moral laws are widely obeyed, life gets better. Where they are not, life gets worse. It's cause and effect, like the laws of physics and chemistry.

Common law was the system for discovering and applying Natural Law in human affairs.

An important point here concerns good intentions. You might have heard the expression, "The road to hell is paved with good intentions."

If you jump out of an airplane without a parachute, you know what will happen. It's cause and effect. Even if you have the best of intentions—even if you are absolutely convinced you can fly like a bird—it won't make any difference. Your intentions cannot repeal Natural Law.

Cause and effect also exists with natural moral laws. When force or fraud enter a transaction, odds are that someone will suffer a loss and civilization will move slightly backward. Intentions do not matter.

Suppose John Q. Citizen is totally convinced that some group of people is in need and John Q. Citizen is therefore entitled to take your money by force to give to them. John Q. Citizen could launch an effort to set up a private charity to help these people, using voluntary means, but let's say he is convinced their need makes the use of force okay.

John Q. Citizen launches a political campaign to persuade the government to take your money and give it to the needy. In this case we will say these needy persons are a large corporation that is going broke and will have to lay off its employees if it isn't rescued.

John Q. Citizen's intentions won't matter. When the money is taken by force, a large number of people, you included, will suffer losses.

Those who suffer will respond. They will now spend much of their time and money trying to avoid these losses. Some will do this legally, engaging in tax avoidance. They will hire accountants, lawyers, and financial advisors to find tax loopholes for them. Vast amounts of time, effort, and wealth will be diverted to unproductive money-shuffling.

Others will do it illegally with tax evasion. They will spend time, effort, and money searching for secret, illegal ways to escape the taxes.

The government will retaliate by expanding the tax bureaucracy to catch them. Some will go to prison, and prisons are expensive. More vast sums of money will be diverted to unproductive activity. Losses will multiply and civilization will move backward. Somewhere, somehow, poverty will increase. It's cause and effect.

The needy corporation and its employees will be better off, and this will be highly visible because this group will be concentrated in a single location. John Q. Citizen will boast about being their benefactor.

But thousands of others will be worse off, although they will be widely scattered and not noticeable. The fact that they are not noticeable will enable John to brag and get away with it. But, despite appearances, civilization will be held back.

Here is an interesting remark by Thomas Paine made in 1792:

> To say that any people are not fit for freedom, is to make poverty their choice, and to say they had rather be loaded with taxes than not.

Notice Paine is saying that without freedom poverty is automatic. Economists today know this is because of economic calculation. When force or fraud enter a transaction, odds are that someone will suffer a loss. This is how the universe is made and we cannot change it. Just like the laws of physics and chemistry.

From this theory of Natural Law came the early Americans' belief in the Natural Rights of the individual. Samuel Adams said:

> The Natural Rights of the colonists are these: first, a right to life; second, to liberty; third, to property; together with the right to support and defend them in the best manner they can.

Because the law that says "do not encroach" is a Natural Law made by the Creator, a person has Natural Rights to his life, liberty, and property granted by the Creator. They are a logical extension, the Founders believed. Samuel Adams did an outstanding job of explaining this in his excellent 1772 essay THE RIGHTS OF THE COLONISTS.[17] I suggest you read it.

Chris, an interesting point here is that the early Americans were very likely the most law-abiding people ever—if we are talking about common law; but if political law, they were rebels from the start.

They came to America specifically to violate the tariffs, trade restrictions, taxes, and religious laws of the government. Virtually every colonist disobeyed these laws. In fact, disobedience to them was the foundation of the economy. Few American industries could have survived if they had paid all the taxes and obeyed all the regulations. John Hancock was known as the Prince of Smugglers.

> *"All men are by nature equally free and independent and have certain inherent rights, of which, when they enter into a state of society, they cannot, by any compact, deprive or divest their posterity; namely, the enjoyment of life and liberty, with the means of acquiring and possessing property, and pursuing and obtaining happiness and safety."*
>
> — *Virginia Declaration of Rights 1776*

But the early Americans were dedicated to the principles of common law. At Lexington, Concord, and other battlefields, hundreds gave their lives for these principles.

To my mind, the very best definition of liberty ever written was by Jefferson:

---

[17] THE REVOLUTIONARY YEARS edited by Mortimer Adler, Encyclopedia Britannica, Chicago, 1976, p. 65-68

Rightful liberty is unobstructed action according to our will within limits drawn around us by the equal rights of others. I do not add "within the limits of the law" because law is often but the tyrant's will, and always so when it violates the rights of the individual.

Obviously, Jefferson pulled that definition straight from the second fundamental law, do not encroach on other persons or their property.

Chris, in my next letter we will continue our discussion of Natural Law. Until then, remember the Founders' belief in Natural Law, and that a person is endowed by his Creator with rights to his life, liberty, and property.

Uncle Eric

John Hancock
"Prince of Smugglers"
Painting by
John Singleton Copley
Reproduced from the
DICTIONARY OF
AMERICAN PORTRAITS,
published by Dover
Publications, Inc., in 1967.

..natural rights provided the moral philosophic under-pinning for the U.S. Declaration of Independence...

During the 19th and early 20th centuries, natural rights fell into disfavor with legal philosophers....

Natural rights theory was largely replaced with legal positivism. Positivism holds that legal authority stems solely from what the state has laid down as law...However, the flaw in positivist philosophy is that the law is no better than the source of its authority.

In the aftermath of World War II, a revival of natural rights theory emerged. It was due in part to the revulsion against Nazism, which revealed the horrors that could emanate from a positivist system...

— Attorney Jerome J. Shestack
former U.S. ambassador to the U.N.
Commission on Human Rights
"There's Nothing Alien About Natural Rights"
WALL STREET JOURNAL, September 6, 1991

14

The Human Ecology

"No arbitrary regulation, no act of the legislature, can add anything to the capital[18] of the country; it can only force it into artificial channels."

— *J.R. McCulloch, economist*
(1789-1864)
PRINCIPLES OF POLITICAL ECONOMY

Dear Chris,

An economy is an ecology. It's not a machine. It's a biological system like a forest or tropical reef, but far more complex. The network of relationships is intricate and fragile. Forcible intervention does damage.

Even if the force is applied with the best of intentions, damage happens.

As in a forest or tropical reef, the consequences of force might not be apparent in the exact location where the force is applied, but it pops up somewhere. You learned this from my previous group of letters about money, inflation, investment cycles, and recessions.[19] The legal tender laws have brought

---

[18] wealth

[19] Uncle Eric is referring to WHATEVER HAPPENED TO PENNY CANDY? by Richard J. Maybury, published by Bluestocking Press, phone: 800-959-8586, web site: www.BluestockingPress.com

America untold hardship, including recessions, depressions, unemployment, and deprivation. The more government we get the more poverty we get.

The two fundamental laws are part of the fabric of the universe, like the laws of physics and chemistry. Where these laws are violated, life gets worse; where they are obeyed, life gets better. It's cause and effect.

Violators, of course, always hope to avoid the consequences themselves. But someone somewhere pays.

Common law was an attempt to insure that the only person who pays is the person who disobeyed. The idea was to protect civilization by preventing the damage from being dispersed— by concentrating it at the point, the individual, who committed the violation.

> "Let not him who is houseless pull down the house of another, but let him work diligently and build one for himself, thus by example assuring that his own one shall be safe from violence when built."
>
> — Abraham Lincoln

Sometimes I think the connection between law and economics was better understood two hundred years ago than it is today. Former U.S. assistant attorney general Charles Warren once drew attention to the sequence of instruction at Harvard Law School in its first decade, 1817-27. Harvard introduced students to law through the works of William Blackstone, then taught them economics. First law, then economics. As I said in my first letter, economics is only a symptom, the cause is law.

Today, knowledge of this connection between law and economics has been almost completely lost. People study either law or economics but rarely both. Even more rarely are they shown how the two are intertwined. Now that you know, I hope you will tell others about economic calculation.

Let me emphasize something that should be obvious but is often ignored. Humans are biological organisms. We are like forest creatures, whales, and all the rest. Our natural system for survival is not an ocean or a rainforest, it is an economy, but an economy is an ecological system every bit as much as these others.

Chris, common law was the system for discovering the Natural Law that governs the human ecology. We can learn this law, obey it, and reap the rewards — or ignore it, our choice. But it's always there producing its inevitable results.

Keep in mind that right and wrong are not matters of opinion. They are principles we must discover and apply. They are laws of biology for intelligent species.

By the way, in a future letter I'll explain how our refusal to use common law has led to the destruction of forests, reefs, and other ecological systems. When humans do not obey the two fundamental laws they foul not only their own ecology but the ecologies of other creatures, too.

Uncle Eric

P.S. In my next letter I'll enclose a treat—a classic story called "I Pencil."

A Two-Sided Coin

The system of liberty is a two-sided coin. Common law was the legal side, and free markets are the economic side.

In a free market, people can produce and sell whatever goods and services they choose.

What guides them to produce what others need? The desire for gain.

In his book THE WEALTH OF NATIONS, the great economist Adam Smith explained that business persons earn money by offering goods others wish to buy. To earn more they must constantly improve these goods so that the goods are in greater demand. This is the so-called "Invisible Hand" that guides free markets to produce what people need.

> By directing that industry in such a manner as its produce may be of the greatest value, he intends only his own gain. ... He is in this, as in many other cases, led by an invisible hand to promote an end which was no part of his intention. ... By pursuing his own interest he frequently promotes that of society more effectually than when he really intends to promote it.
>
> — Adam Smith
> THE WEALTH OF NATIONS

15

How Things Get Done

Dear Chris,

Under the principles of common law, how do people organize themselves? How do things get done?

By applying the first law, they use voluntary agreements: one individual's simple offer, "If you will do this for me, I will do that for you," and another's answer, "I agree."

The best explanation ever written was by Leonard Read of the Foundation for Economic Education. His essay, I PENCIL, is a classic. Enjoy.

Uncle Eric

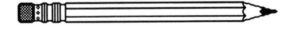

No one knows how to make a pencil.

I, Pencil

by Leonard E. Read

(reprinted by permission of the Foundation for Economic Education, Inc., Irvington-on-Hudson, New York 10533)

To summarize the philosophy of freedom and marvel at the results, one must wonder at the mystery of the creation of so simple an item as a lead pencil.

Here is a pencil's story as told to Leonard Read in 1958. The pencil's official name is "Mongol 482." Its many ingredients are assembled, fabricated, and finished in Eberhard Faber Pencil Company, Wilkes-Barre, Pennsylvania.

I am a lead pencil—the ordinary wooden pencil familiar to all boys and girls and adults who can read and write. Writing is both my vocation and my avocation; that's all I do.

You may wonder why I should write a genealogy. Well, to begin with, my story is interesting. And, next, I am a mystery—more so than a tree or a sunset or even a flash of lightning. But, sadly, I am taken for granted by those who use me, as if I were a mere incident and without background. This supercilious attitude relegates me to the level of the commonplace. This is a species of the grievous error in which mankind cannot too long persist without peril. For, the wise G. K. Chesterton observed, "We are perishing for want of wonder, not for want of wonders."

I, Pencil, simple though I appear to be, merit your wonder and awe, a claim I shall attempt to prove. In fact, if you can understand me—no, that's too much to ask of anyone—if you can become aware of the miraculousness which I symbolize, you can help save the freedom mankind is so unhappily losing. I have a profound lesson to teach. And I can teach this lesson better than can an automobile or an airplane or a mechanical dishwasher because—well, because I am seemingly so simple.

Simple? Yet, *not a single person on the face of this earth knows how to make me.* This sounds fantastic, doesn't it? Especially when it is realized that there are about one and one-half billion of my kind produced in the U.S.A. each year.

Pick me up and look me over. What do you see? Not much meets the eye—there's some wood, lacquer, the printed labeling, graphite lead, a bit of metal, and an eraser.

Innumerable Antecedents

Just as you cannot trace your family tree back very far, so is it impossible for me to name and explain all my antecedents. But I would like to suggest enough of them to impress upon you the richness and complexity of my background.

My family tree begins with what in fact is a tree, a cedar of straight grain that grows in Northern California and Oregon. Now contemplate all the saws and trucks and rope and the countless other gear used in harvesting and carting the cedar logs to the railroad siding. Think of all the persons and the numberless skills that went into their fabrication: the mining of ore, the making of steel and its refinement into saws, axes, motors; the growing of hemp and bringing it through all the stages to heavy and strong rope; the logging camps with their beds and mess halls, the cookery and the raising of all the foods. Why, untold thousands of persons had a hand in every cup of coffee the loggers drink!

The logs are shipped to a mill in San Leandro, California. Can you imagine the individuals who make flat cars and rails and railroad engines and who construct and install the communication systems incidental thereto? These legions are among my antecedents.

Consider the millwork in San Leandro. The cedar logs are cut into small, pencil-length slats less than one-fourth of an inch in thickness. These are kiln dried and then tinted for the same reason women put rouge on their faces. People prefer that I look pretty, not a pallid white. The slats are waxed and kiln dried again. How many skills went into the making of the tint and the kilns, into supplying the heat, the light and power, the belts, motors, and all the other things a mill requires? Sweepers in the mill among my ancestors? Yes, and included are the men who poured the concrete for the dam of a Pacific Gas & Electric Company hydroplant which supplies the mill's power!

Don't overlook the ancestors present and distant who have a hand in transporting sixty carloads of slats across the nation from California to Wilkes-Barre!

Complicated Machinery

Once in the pencil factory—$4,000,000 in machinery and building, all capital accumulated by thrifty and saving parents of mine—each slat is given eight grooves by a complex machine, after which another machine lays leads in every other slat, applies glue, and places another slat atop—a lead sandwich, so to speak. Seven brothers and I are mechanically carved from this "wood-clinched" sandwich.

My "lead" itself—it contains no lead at all—is complex. The graphite is mined in Sri Lanka. Consider these miners and those who make their many tools and the makers of the paper sacks in which the graphite is shipped and those who make the string that ties the sacks and those who put them aboard ships and those who make the ships. Even the lighthouse keepers along the way assisted in my birth—and the harbor pilots.

The graphite is mixed with clay from Mississippi in which ammonium hydroxide is used in the refining process. Then wetting agents are added such as sulfonated tallow—animal fats chemically reacted with sulfuric acid. After passing through numerous machines, the mixture finally appears as endless extrusions—as from a sausage grinder—cut to size, dried, and baked for several hours at 1,850 degrees Fahrenheit. To increase their strength and smoothness the leads are then treated with a hot mixture which includes candelilla wax from Mexico, paraffin wax, and hydrogenated natural fats.

My cedar receives six coats of lacquer. Do you know all of the ingredients of lacquer? Who would think that the growers of castor beans and the refiners of castor oil are a part of it? They are. Why, even the processes by which the lacquer is made a beautiful yellow involve the skills of more persons than one can enumerate!

Observe the labeling. That's a film formed by applying heat to carbon black mixed with resins. How do you make resins and what, pray, is carbon black?

My bit of metal—the ferrule—is brass. Think of all the persons who mine zinc and copper and those who have the skills to make shiny sheet brass from these products of nature. Those black rings on my ferrule are black nickel. What is black nickel and how is it applied? The complete story of why the center of my ferrule has no black nickel on it would take pages to explain.

Then there's my crowning glory, inelegantly referred to in the trade as "the plug," the part man uses to erase the errors he makes with me. An ingredient called "factice" is what does the erasing. It is a rubber-like product made by reacting rape seed oil from the Dutch East Indies with sulfur chloride. Rubber, contrary to the common notion, is only for binding purposes. Then, too, there are numerous vulcanizing and accelerating agents. The pumice comes from Italy; and the pigment which gives "the plug" its color is cadmium sulfide.

No One Knows

Does anyone wish to challenge my earlier assertion that no single person on the face of this earth knows how to make me?

Actually, millions of human beings have had a hand in my creation, no one of whom even knows more than a very few of the others. Now, you may say that I go too far in relating the picker of a coffee berry in far off Brazil and food growers elsewhere to my creation, that this is an extreme position. I shall stand by my claim. There isn't a single person in all these millions, including the president of the pencil company, who contributes more than a tiny, infinitesimal bit of know-how. From the standpoint of know-how the only difference between the miner of graphite in Sri Lanka and the logger in Oregon is in the *type* of know-how. Neither the miner nor the logger can be dispensed with, any more than can the chemist at the factory or the worker in the oil field—paraffin being a by-product of petroleum.

Here is an astounding fact: Neither the worker in the oil field nor the chemist nor the digger of graphite or clay nor any who mans or makes the ships or trains or trucks nor the one who runs the machine that does the knurling on my bit of metal nor the president of the company performs his singular task because he wants me. Each one wants me less, perhaps, than does a child in the first grade. Indeed, there are some among this vast multitude who never saw a pencil nor would they know how to use one. Their motivation is other than me. Perhaps it is something like this: Each of these millions sees that he can thus exchange his tiny know-how for the goods and services he needs or wants. I may or may not be among these items.

No Master Mind

There is a fact still more astounding: the absence of a master mind, of anyone dictating or forcibly directing these countless actions which bring me into being. No trace of such a person can be found. Instead, we find the Invisible Hand at work. This is the mystery to which I earlier referred.

It has been said that "only God can make a tree." Why do we agree with this? Isn't it because we realize that we ourselves could not make one? Indeed, can we even describe a tree? We cannot, except in superficial terms. We can say, for instance, that a certain molecular configuration manifests itself as a tree. But what mind is there among men that could even record, let alone direct, the constant changes in molecules that transpire in the life span of a tree? Such a feat is utterly unthinkable!

I, Pencil, am a complex combination of miracles: a tree, zinc, copper, graphite, and so on. But to these miracles which manifest themselves in Nature an even more extraordinary miracle has been added: the configuration of creative human energies—millions of tiny know-hows configurating naturally and spontaneously in response to human necessity and desire and *in the absence of any human masterminding!* Since only God can make a tree, I insist that only God could make me. Man can no more direct these millions of know-hows to bring me into being than he can put molecules together to create a tree.

The above is what I meant when writing, "If you can become aware of the miraculousness which I symbolize, you can help save the freedom mankind is so unhappily losing." For, if one is aware that these know-hows will naturally, yes, automatically, arrange themselves into creative and productive patterns in response to human necessity and demand—that is, in the absence of governmental or any other coercive master-minding—then one will possess an absolutely essential ingredient for freedom: *a faith in free men.* Freedom is impossible without this faith.

Once government has had a monopoly of a creative activity such, for instance, as the delivery of the mails, most individuals will believe that the mails could not be efficiently delivered by men acting freely. And here is the reason: Each one acknowledges that he himself doesn't know how to do all the things incident to mail delivery. He also recognizes that no other individual could do it. These assumptions are correct. No individual possesses enough know-how to perform a nation's mail delivery any more than any individual possesses enough know-how to make a pencil. Now, in the absence of faith in free men—in the unawareness that millions of tiny know-hows would naturally and miraculously form and cooperate to satisfy this necessity—the individual cannot help but reach the erroneous conclusion that mail can be delivered only be governmental "master-minding."

Testimony Galore

If I, Pencil, were the only item that could offer testimony on what men can accomplish when free to try, then those with little faith would have a fair case. However, there is testimony galore; it's all about us and on every hand. Mail delivery is exceedingly simple when compared, for instance, to the making of an automobile or a calculator or a grain combine or a milling machine or to tens of thousands of other things.

The lesson I have to teach is this: *Leave all creative energies uninhibited.* Merely organize society to act in harmony with this lesson. Let society's legal apparatus remove all obstacles the best it can. Permit these creative know-hows freely to flow. Have faith that free men will respond to the Invisible Hand. This faith will be confirmed. I, Pencil, seemingly simple though I am, offer the miracle of my creation as testimony that this is a practical faith, as practical as the sun, the rain, a cedar tree, the good earth.

No one knows how to make a pencil.

"*Were we directed from Washington when to sow, and when to reap, we should soon want bread.*"
— Thomas Jefferson, 1821

16

Political Law

Dear Chris,

Now we'll get into **political law**. This is the law we have today. It is *made up* law, created out of nothing. Whatever the powerholders say, is law. And if they change their minds, the law changes.

During the twentieth century the entire world had been switching over to political law, and now the transition is almost complete.

This transition has many causes. Perhaps the most important was the Great Depression of the 1930s. In those days people didn't understand enough economics to know the depression was caused by inflation. You and many others understand this today,[20] but only a handful knew it then.

Not understanding the cause, they became desperate and frightened. They demanded their governments do something, anything, even if this meant a massive expansion of the use of force on persons who had not harmed anyone. Political law swept the world.

In an attempt to stop the depression, governments flooded

---

[20] Explained in WHATEVER HAPPENED TO PENNY CANDY? by Richard J. Maybury, published by Bluestocking Press, phone: 800-959-8586, web site: www.BluestockingPress.com

the earth with new laws. It was one legal experiment after another, with very little regard for the two fundamental laws.

As you have probably already guessed, political law isn't just a different kind of law from the old common law, it is the opposite. It is based on political power—on brute force—not on the two fundamental laws; it's crude and primitive.

Political law has no requirement for logic or morality. It changes whenever the political wind changes. Fickle and tangled, no one understands it.

Democracy or dictatorship, it doesn't matter, political law is arbitrary. You do whatever the powerholders say, or else, even if it's morally wrong.

This is why majority rule has so often become mob rule. Remember the Reign of Terror growing out of the French Revolution? The Salem witch trials? The U.S. Government's slaughter of the Native Americans?

The majority is as human as any dictator. Like the dictator, they do not vote for what is right, they vote for what they want.

Their wants change constantly, so political law has no stability. It destroys investors' and businessmen's ability to plan ahead. Economic progress becomes very difficult.

Imagine trying to play a game of baseball while the audience is voting every few minutes to change the rules. This is the situation employers and investors are in now.

How the law has changed. In 1897, Supreme Court Justice Oliver Wendell Holmes, Jr. defined law as "systemized prediction." He said, "The prophecies of what the courts will do in fact, and nothing more pretentious, are what I mean by the law."[21] Now, no one has the slightest idea what the courts will do, the law changes daily.

---

[21] "The Path of the Law," by Oliver Wendell Holmes, Jr., LAW, edited by Sara Robbins, Macmillan Publishing, New York, 1990, pg. 276.

America's Founders understood the dangers of political law. James Madison asked in THE FEDERALIST PAPERS,

> What prudent merchant will hazard his fortunes in any new branch of commerce when he knows not that his plans may be rendered unlawful before they can be executed?

When merchants do not hazard their fortunes, new businesses are not created and workers are not hired. We get more unemployment and poverty.

The American Revolution was fought over the difference between scientific law and political law. Government officials had been expanding their encroachment into the private businesses, lives, and property of the colonists. The colonists said the officials had no right to do this. "All men are created equal." God has given no one special permission to encroach on others. No one, not even government officials. Thomas Jefferson:

> *"A recent survey by the Conference Board, a group of 3600 organizations in more than 50 nations, reports that for fear of civil liability:*
> *• 47% of U.S. manufacturers have withdrawn products from the market;*
> *• 25% of U.S. manufacturers have discontinued some forms of product research;*
> *• Approximately 15% of U.S. companies have laid off workers as a direct result of product liability experience."*
>
> — WALL STREET JOURNAL
> *August 14, 1991*

> The general spread of the light of science has already laid open to every view the palpable truth that the mass of mankind has not been born with saddles on their

backs, nor a favored few booted and spurred, ready to ride them legitimately by the grace of God.

In one of the earlier attempts to state the two fundamental laws, Jefferson made this remark in 1809:

Reading, reflection, and time have convinced me that the interests of society require the observation of those moral precepts only in which all religions agree, for all forbid us to murder, steal, plunder, or bear false witness.

The Founders believed the principles of the old common law were superior to political law. After the revolution, they created the Bill of Rights and other documents based on these ancient principles. The goal was to make the superiority of these principles permanent and to keep officials restrained by them.

But during this century the restraints have been broken. All we have left is political law. We are forced to do whatever the voters or their elected representatives say.

Chris, this is a good place to introduce an extremely important clergyman named Jonathan Mayhew, whom President John Adams called a "transcendent genius."[22] In 1750, Mayhew gave a sermon that Adams said, "was read by everybody."[23]

The sermon was a deep exploration of religious principles relating to the authority of human governments. In it, Mayhew described what the government was doing and

[22] THE REVOLUTIONARY YEARS by Mortimer J. Adler, Encyclopedia Britannica, Chicago, 1976, p. 21 and 306.
[23] Ibid.

pointed out that this violated Higher Law. He told the audience that a king's authority is legitimate when the king obeys Higher Law, but when the king...

> ...turns tyrant and makes his subjects his prey to devour and to destroy instead of his charge to defend and cherish, we are bound to throw off our allegiance to him and to resist.[24]

Mayhew pulled no punches:

> We may safely assert...that no civil rulers are to be obeyed when they enjoin things that are inconsistent with the commands of God. ... All commands running counter to the declared will of the supreme legislator of heaven and earth, are null and void; and therefore disobedience to them is a duty, not a crime.[25]

Not just the king, "no civil rulers," said Mayhew, are to be obeyed if their rules are inconsistent with "the commands of God."

According to John Adams, this sermon was the real beginning of the American Revolution. It showed the people that they had to choose between their God's law and their government's law.[26] Fortunately, enough had the courage to choose the path Adams chose, and this led to creation of the most free and prosperous nation ever seen on earth.

---

[24] Ibid.

[25] Ibid.

[26] For a copy of this sermon and John Adams' remarks about it, contact Bluestocking Press, web site: www.BluestockingPress.com, phone: 800-959-8586.

President John Quincy Adams once explained that, "the virtue which had been infused into the Constitution of the United States, and was to give to its vital existence" was that it would be "always subordinate to a rule of right and wrong, and always responsible to the Supreme Ruler of the universe."[27]

Americans today sometimes assume the Founders' references to God or Nature or the Supreme Ruler were just for impact or for propaganda. Not so. These were tightly reasoned statements of legal principles. Your rights to your life, liberty, and property came from your Creator, not the government; these rights cannot be repealed.

> *"The legislative has no right to absolute, arbitrary power over the lives and fortunes of the people; nor can mortals assume a prerogative not only too high for men, but for angels, and therefore reserved for the exercise of the Deity alone."*
>
> *— Samuel Adams*
> RIGHTS OF THE COLONISTS,
> *November 20, 1772*

Chris, in my next letter I'll tell you more about the differences between political law and scientific law, or common law. Until then, remember two points: (1) political law has no requirement for logic or morality, and (2) it changes any time powerholders wish to change it, which means constantly; we cannot plan ahead.

Uncle Eric

---

[27] THE REVOLUTIONARY YEARS, Ibid.

If there is a single reason for my immigration to the U.S. it would be the two complementing documents of the Constitution and Bill of Rights. ...

I am always surprised by my fellow citizens born in America because they take these documents for granted and do not put those principles into practice.

I have traveled and studied in more than 50 countries. I always come back to the U.S. and I'm glad to come home. Nothing's better than home: America.

> Makram Samman (originally from Egypt)
> Letter to the SACRAMENTO BEE newspaper,
> published August 4, 1991

17

Discovery vs. Enactment

"The more laws, the less justice."
— *German Proverb*

Dear Chris,

Let's return to Thomas Paine's remark, "Man cannot make principles, he can only discover them." Common law was a process of discovery. There were courts before there was law. If you remember nothing else from my letters, remember that. The court came first, then came the common law, which was an attempt to reflect Natural Law.

Just like physics and chemistry. First comes the scientist, then comes the equations and formulas.

Notice that the equations and formulas are not the laws of physics or chemistry, they are only approximations. Scientists are always trying to make them more accurate.

The same with common law. The judges believed there was a law higher than any human law, and they were trying to discover and apply this Higher Law. It was being carefully, logically worked out, case by case, century after century, exactly like the laws of physics and chemistry. Common law was the result—the equations and formulas.

Compare this process to the efforts made by your own parents, Chris. They are always asking themselves, "What's fair?" As they learn, rules are improved.

Your parents are not trying to create rules out of nothing. They don't ask, "What should I make right?" They ask, "What is right, and what should I do about it?" Right and wrong already exist; your parents would be shocked if someone suggested they had the power to change them.

I've long felt that parenting would be much easier if parents knew common law. Most serious problems arising from human relationships were worked out centuries ago in the common law courts. Common law was packed with helpful insights. Without it, parents today are reinventing the wheel. (Parents, see Suggested Reading in the Appendix.)

When Ludwig von Mises, F. A. Hayek, and other economists discovered the connection between law and economic calculation, this was like Newton's flash of insight about gravity when he saw the apple fall from the tree. "So that's how the world works!" See Mises' short article "Economic Calculation in a Socialist Commonwealth," and his books SOCIALISM and PLANNED CHAOS. Also see Hayek's Nobel Prize winning book ROAD TO SERFDOM. At the time I write this, some or all of these are available from either the Foundation for Economic Education or Bluestocking Press.

Political law, on the other hand, is an enactment process. Legislators—lawmakers—make changes according to whatever political pressures they happen to be feeling at the moment. Something that is right today can be wrong tomorrow and right again the next day. There are no eternal truths and no interest in discovering Natural Law.

Political law is shallow.

Under political law the frequent changing of right and wrong is considered good. Running for re-election, lawmakers proudly boast of the number of new laws they have enacted.

In short, we now live in a world where it is assumed politicians have the divine power to make up law; they have become deities. In 1788, Patrick Henry realized this could happen. During his struggle to prevent the creation of the Federal Government[28] he warned that "Congress, from their general powers, may fully go into the business of human legislation." Henry's warning was ignored and few people today see human legislation as the primitive and arbitrary system that it is.

BUSINESS WEEK says that each year in the U.S. there are more than 100,000 new laws, rules, and regulations enacted. This is the most important reason the economy is becoming so rickety. Tax rates, money supply, trade restrictions, licensing laws, and thousands of other business ground rules are forever being stirred around like a witch's brew. This causes money to slosh from one area to another in unpredictable ways. Employers can't plan ahead.

A study done a few years ago showed that between 1976 and 1986, state legislatures made up 248,000 new laws. On average each of these laws spawned at least ten new regulations that have the force of law. This means, in effect, the state legislatures alone made up more than two million new laws.[29] Think about it. Two million new laws! And this doesn't include laws made by federal and local officials.

---

[28] Few Americans today remember anything about Patrick Henry and the Anti-Federalists. A good introduction is THE ANTI-FEDERALISTS by Jackson Turner Main, W.W. Norton & Co., 1961.

[29] "Prolific Part-Timers in the Statehouses," by Robert S. McCord, WALL STREET JOURNAL, January 21, 1987, p. 22.

If you break one, remember ignorance of the law is no excuse.

It will be of little avail to the people that the laws are made by men of their own choice if the laws be so voluminous that they cannot be read, or so incoherent that they cannot be understood.

> — James Madison
> Federalist Paper #62

We have ten times more laws than our great-grandparents had.

> — Robert S. McCord
> WALL STREET JOURNAL
> January 21, 1987

Imagine if a scientist claimed he had *made up* a law of physics or chemistry. He'd be carted away to a lunatic asylum.

As we'd expect, much of political law is complete fantasy. In THE TRENTON PICKLE ORDINANCE AND OTHER BONEHEAD LEGISLATION, journalist Dick Hyman cites 600 examples of America's political law.

> *"The world's businessmen understand that the U.S. legal system is a running joke, and trade tales that start, have-you-heard-this-one-yet?"*
>
> — WALL STREET JOURNAL *editorial*
> *August 14, 1991*

In Massachusetts, says Hyman, it is illegal to put tomatoes in clam chowder. In South Carolina you are breaking the law if your trousers have hip pockets. In Vermont it is against the law to whistle under water.

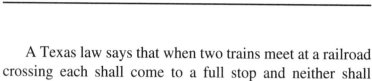

A Texas law says that when two trains meet at a railroad crossing each shall come to a full stop and neither shall proceed until the other has gone.

My favorite is this: The Arkansas legislature once enacted a law forbidding the Arkansas River to rise higher than the Main Street bridge in Little Rock.

Did you laugh at these examples? Think about this. You were laughing at the law.

If decent, honest Americans will laugh at the law, how can we expect anyone else to take it seriously? I sometimes fear we are much closer to chaos than we realize.

Go back to my seventh letter and reread Edmund Burke's remark about our forefathers' study of law. Burke refers to this law as a science. Would any sane person today call our law a science?

Human legislation is arbitrary and primitive. It belongs to the era of stone knives and bearskins. But it has been revived, and it now rules our modern world of computers, lasers, and space satellites.

Imagine a cave man at the controls of a Boeing 747. This is our situation.

Medical doctor Ron Paul has spent more than six terms in Congress. In a conversation he once told me that many proposed laws are hundreds of pages long, and few are read by lawmakers before they are voted on—there isn't time. Think about that. Lawmakers themselves are ignorant of the laws they make up.

Dr. Paul once proposed a new rule for the House. Before voting, a lawmaker would have been required to sign a statement saying (1) he had read the proposed law, (2) he understood it, and (3) he knew a way to finance it. The rule was rejected.

Chris, until my next letter, remember that the old common law was discovered law. There were courts before there was law. Political law is made up law, created out of nothing.

Uncle Eric

James Madison
Painting by Gilbert Stuart
Reproduced from the DICTIONARY OF AMERICAN PORTRAITS,
published by Dover Publications, Inc., in 1967.

"It will be of little avail to the people that the laws are made by men of their own choice if the laws be so voluminous that they cannot be read, or so incoherent that they cannot be understood."

— James Madison
Federalist Paper #62

It is utterly irreconcilable to these principles and to many other fundamental maxims of the common law, common sense, and reason that a British House of Commons [legislature] should have a right at pleasure to give and grant the property of the colonists.

— Samuel Adams
RIGHTS OF THE COLONISTS,
November 20, 1772

Somewhere along the way things began to go awry. The problem is law. Somehow we moved from being an innovative, creative and dynamic society to becoming the most litigious people on earth. ... There are more students in law schools than in all the graduate schools in engineering, chemistry, physics and the biological sciences combined.

— Paul F. Oreffice, CEO
Dow Chemical
IMPRIMIS published by
Hillsdale College, July 1987

18

Our New Religion

Dear Chris,

In case you are wondering, there are practical everyday reasons for understanding the difference between common law and political law. It can affect your pocketbook. In 1984 I wrote a special report, INVESTMENT FRAUDS, RIP-OFFS AND CONS,[30] to help investors avoid swindlers. Here is an excerpt from the introduction:

> A major requirement for successful investing is the constant awareness that there is a new religion in the world. The god of this new religion is government, and the ritual the worshippers perform is legislation. Faith in this new religion is deep and profound. The worshippers are convinced their god can solve almost any problem, if only the right legislation can be performed.
>
> This new religion is so popular you could probably make a strong case that it is replacing the old religions. It's even been embraced by people who should

---

[30] Published by World Perspective Communications, Orlando, FL.

know better. These people are like the economist described by author Gita Meitta in her book KARMA COLA. The economist felt the need for spiritual guidance, so she flew to India to consult with a Hindu guru. The consultation did not yield the desired guidance, however, and the economist reacted by complaining that the Indian government "should definitely have a quality control on gurus."

There is an abundance of legislation for every problem known to mankind, especially financial problems. The worshippers are convinced this legislation is truly protecting them against financial rip-offs, so they feel less need to protect themselves.

The ritual does not work. The god is a false god, and we are on our own.

Many years have passed since I wrote those words, but today I believe them more than ever. Political law has become the world's new religion and it is replacing the old ones. Legislators have become priests, and capitol buildings have become temples. None of it has the slightest connection with reality.

> "It is not desirable to cultivate a respect for the law so much as for the right."
>
> — Henry David Thoreau
> 1849

I remember visiting the state capitol building in Sacramento. The interior resembles a cathedral. I had the strangest compulsion to keep my head bowed, to speak in whispers, and kneel.

This new religion is more entrenched in America than anywhere else. Our tendency to use law for every problem has become so strong that our demand for lawyers has become insatiable. No one knows how many lawyers there are in the U.S., a common estimate is one million. A study done in 1991 found that America had five percent of the world's population but seventy percent of the lawyers,[31] and Americans were filing 18 million lawsuits per year.[32]

All of it involves force. As Alexander Hamilton wrote in Federalist Paper #15,

> It is essential to the idea of a law that it be attended with a sanction; or, in other words, a penalty or punishment for disobedience. If there be no penalty annexed to disobedience, the resolutions or commands which pretend to be laws will, in fact, amount to nothing more than advice or recommendation.

This is why, in a civilized society, law is the last resort, the measure used only after everything else has been tried.

In America today law has become the first resort. Americans have decided: why use a peaceful handshake to solve a problem when you can use a **blackjack**?

Chris, do not be fooled into thinking you are safe from rip-offs just because they are illegal. Protection of innocent persons is now just one of the hundreds of purposes of law. It probably isn't even a top priority any more.

Uncle Eric

---

[31] WALL STREET JOURNAL, August 14, 1991, p. A10
[32] Ibid.

Lawsuits Commenced in Federal District Courts

(source: STATISTICAL ABSTRACT OF THE UNITED STATES)

Year	Number of Filings
1950	44,454
1960	59,284
1970	87,321
1980	168,789
1990	217,879
2000	263,049

Our New Temple
Law has become a religious ritual for solving any problem.

19

Common Law Wasn't Perfect

"Unnecessary laws are not good laws, but traps for money."

—*Thomas Hobbes*
LEVIATHAN, *1651*

Dear Chris,

Please don't get the impression I'm arguing for a straight-forward return to the old common law. This would be an outrageous idea that would raise eyebrows among legal scholars everywhere.

Common law wasn't perfect. Far from it. Overlaid by centuries of political tinkering—by the blackjack mentality—it was a bit crazy in places. Even the American Founders were somewhat skeptical of it. In Federalist Paper #15 Hamilton praised Americans:

Is it not the glory of the people of America that, whilst they have paid a decent regard to the opinions of former times and other nations, they have not suffered a blind veneration for antiquity, for custom or for names, to overrule the suggestions of their own good sense, the knowledge of their own situation, and the lessons of their experience?

Obviously, one of the craziest parts of common law was the ruling added in later centuries that it could be changed by statutes — by political law. This was an exact contradiction of everything common law stood for. It was like a physicist saying $E=MC^2$ is the law of relativity until we vote to change it. Not very bright.

This belief that statutes can override common law came from the belief in majority rule. If the majority or their representatives vote for something, this makes it ethical, right?

Well, I don't think so, but that's the foundation of law today.

We need to return to common law, yes, but to a purer form, one more tightly bound to the two fundamental laws. For many issues, the courts need to start fresh, at the point where all major religions and philosophies agree. They need to build up new case law—new precedents—from there. Do all you have agreed to do, and do not encroach on other persons or their property.

Incidentally, I always try to say "major" religions and philosophies. Every culture has cults and individuals who believe force used on the innocent is fine if it's done for good reasons. I suppose for these persons all that could be done is to point out to them that if they don't like our law they can always choose to be outside it.

Let's look a little closer at the imperfections in the common law.

The origin of common law was in the Dark Ages, a time of ignorance and superstition. Parts of this ignorance and superstition remained until modern times. As late as a hundred years ago, women were not considered fully equal. Skin color had a lot to do with determining a person's guilt or innocence.

Courts of **equity** were invented to correct some of these ancient distortions. These courts were required to place principle above precedent. They did make some effective repairs to the common law. In most of America, equity and common law were eventually merged into one system.

Another reason repairs were needed is that throughout its history the common law had been under assault by political lawmakers who objected to the "do not encroach" law. They thought they were above this rule. Common law judges who said no one was above the law were sometimes persecuted when they refused to enforce political law. More political precedents crept in.

In medieval England so many judges refused to enforce political law that lawmakers invented a whole new court system. This was the Star Chamber which used torture and murder to enforce the politicians' whims.

So, despite efforts to maintain the integrity of common law, as the centuries passed it was gradually overlaid by political law. This layer of political law grew thicker until the 1930s when real common law was completely overwhelmed.

But until the 1930s, common law worked well most of the time. It was a conscious effort aimed in a specific direction—truth and justice—and the people understood it and supported it. It was based on their religious beliefs. Also, it was mostly logical and its aims were moral. It tried to avoid using the blackjack.

Political law has no aim other than to obtain and use political power for whatever the powerholders decide.

Common law was the most advanced legal system ever known and it gave birth to America's founding philosophy. Its principles were those the Minutemen and Sons of Liberty were fighting for in the 1776 American Revolution, and which formed the basis of the Bill of Rights.

I should point out that if you talk to people about common law, you'll find many advocates of political law who have been taught misconceptions about common law.

One of America's top economists once said to me that no serious person could believe in common law because it was so crazy. As an example, he pointed to the early years of the common law when chemistry and other sciences were not available for scientific proofs of innocence and guilt. To decide cases, the plaintiff and defendant engaged in combat. The assumption in those days was that God would strengthen the arm of the innocent. The economist laughed at this primitive notion, and asked if I would want to live under a legal system so barbaric.

Trial by combat did exist in early common law, it's true. But a bit of research sheds more light on the matter. In the excellent classic EXTRAORDINARY POPULAR DELUSIONS AND THE MADNESS OF CROWDS published in 1841, law professor Charles Mackay wrote:

> The clergy, whose dominion was an intellectual one, never approved of a system of jurisprudence which tended so much to bring all things under the rule of the strongest arm. From the first they set their faces against dueling, and endeavored, as far as the prejudices of their age would allow them, to curb the

warlike spirit, so alien from principles of religion. In the Council of Valentia, and afterwards in the Council of Trent, they excommunicated all persons engaged in dueling; and not only them, but even the assistants and spectators, declaring the custom to be hellish and detestable, and introduced by the devil for the destruction both of body and soul. They added also, that princes who connived at duels should be deprived of all temporal power.

Certainly a different picture of common law than the economist had been given, yes? If you haven't read Mackay's book please do so, it's great.

Chris, in my next letter we'll look more closely at political law. Until then, remember that common law wasn't perfect. It had many flaws, but it was the best mankind had done so far.

Uncle Eric

> *"The respective colonies are entitled to the common law of England, and more especially to the great and inestimable privilege of being tried by their peers of the vicinage[33] according to the course of that law."*
>
> — *Continental Congress*
> *October 14, 1774*

---

[33] Local area.

20

Liberty vs. Permission

Dear Chris,

Today's law assumes rights can be granted by the government. However, what the government gives it can also take away. So, under political law we have no real rights and no real liberty, only permissions.

We do not have freedom of speech, we have permission to speak. We do not have freedom of the press, we have permission to publish. Whatever free trade we have left is only permission to trade.

These permissions can be revoked any time the power-holders decide to revoke them. Majority rule.

Courts today do not seek justice, they enforce law. The courts have no concept of justice—no notion of right and wrong—except whatever the law says.

There was a day when two people who had a disagreement would say, "We'll let a court decide." Today the suggestion of a lawsuit is a threat, an act of aggression. Everyone knows that the expense of a lawsuit will be outrageous and the outcome based not on known principles but on the whims of an arbitrary legal system.

The notion that an innocent person has nothing to worry about is laughable. We all know people who have been dragged into court and seriously mistreated, perhaps even bankrupted by the cost, even though they had done nothing to harm anyone.

In short, to threaten a lawsuit is, itself, an assault.

Today's legal system is not a way to prevent harm, it is a way to cause it. It's a weapon.

Under political law we do not have any more genuine liberty than did the Soviets. Our "rights" can be erased.

Under scientific law, the individual's fundamental rights to his life, liberty, and property were held to be

> *"Every fence that the wisdom of our British ancestors had carefully erected against arbitrary power has been violently thrown down."*
>
> — *John Jay*
> ADDRESS TO THE PEOPLE OF BRITAIN
> *October 1774*

gifts granted by the Creator, not by government. These rights could not be erased. Says Arthur R. Hogue in ORIGINS OF THE COMMON LAW, "The common law is marked by a doctrine of the supremacy of law. ... All agencies of government must act upon established principles. ... The king, like his subjects, was under the law."

Attempts to rescue our civilization will fail if we continue living under political law, that is, under the blackjack mentality. Even if hundreds of free market politicians were elected and sweeping free market reforms were enacted, all these reforms could be reversed when the next group of politicians came to power.

Chris, until my next letter remember that under political law we have no genuine liberties, only permissions, and these permissions can be revoked. Majority rule. Law itself has become a weapon.

I'm sure this raises many questions about democracy. Why did the Founders choose majority rule?

We will cover that in a future letter about the nature and behavior of government.

Uncle Eric

John Jay
co-author, THE FEDERALIST; first Chief Justice of U.S.
Painting by Gilbert Stuart
Reproduced from the DICTIONARY OF AMERICAN PORTRAITS,
published by Dover Publications, Inc., in 1967.

"Every fence that the wisdom of our British ancestors had carefully erected against arbitrary power has been violently thrown down."

—John Jay

Innocent or Guilty?

What are right and wrong? What are innocence and guilt?

The Underground Railroad

Prior to the Civil War, slaves escaped from their owners through the help of the so-called Underground Railroad. This was an organization of Americans who hid the slaves, smuggled them north, and showed them how to reach safety in Canada.

Under U.S. law, the Underground Railroad was illegal.

Were Americans who were involved in the Underground Railroad innocent or guilty?

If you had been on a jury, how would you have decided?

The Indian Wars

Prior to the 20th century, the U.S. government sent troops to capture and kill Native Americans. Sometimes entire villages were wiped out—every man, woman, and child put to death.

If a soldier refused to follow orders to do this killing, he was breaking the law.

Was he innocent or guilty?

If you had been on a jury, how would you have decided?

21

Instability, Nuremberg, and Abortion

Dear Chris,

The primitive notion that humans can make law has become ingrained in our culture. In a 1986 WALL STREET JOURNAL article,[34] Justice Department public affairs director Terry Eastland wrote,

> Until this century the jurisprudence prevailing since the U.S. founding insisted on a core of principles in the law that were knowable and could be applied in specific cases by judges. In the first decades of this century dissents from the view became more and more frequent. By the 1930s, the idea of the judge as an interpreter of established law had been almost totally rejected. As a result of the work of the Legal Realists and others, a new perspective developed — that the law is not found by judges, but is made by their interpretations of constitutions and statutes.

One terrible result of this idea that law can be made is complete instability in the law. We don't know who is responsible for what.

---

[34] January 10, 1986.

This disaster has been described by American Insurance Association Vice President Dennis Connolly.[35] "The system is changing," says Connolly, "so that it is no longer possible to predict the responsibility of parties for actions which create injuries, and it is no longer possible to ascertain who will pay for what injuries."

Legal scholar Victor Schwartz adds, "There isn't one rule of law that's stable. There is no rule of law that we can assume will be the same three or four years from now."[36] We can't plan ahead.

Lawmaking is the reason the abortion question may be the most important question in all of American history. I do not exaggerate. Here's the story.

The second fundamental law, do not encroach on other persons or their property, requires a definition of persons. What is a person?

The question may sound silly, but it has long been one of the most important and difficult to answer. Who has a right to life?

In centuries past, when women were property and blacks were slaves, the answer was not so clear. But legal scholars labored away until finally, by this century, almost everyone recognized that if white males have a right to life, so do women and blacks. We are all created equal.

Unfortunately, this is as far as the common law progressed before it was overwhelmed by political law. Many questions about rights to liberty and property, especially the liberty and property of children, remain unanswered. Or they are answered arbitrarily by political law, majority rule.

Also unanswered are right-to-life questions related to animals and fetuses. We know the right to life is somehow

---

[35] *ABC Nightline*, December 26, 1985.
[36] Ibid.

connected to intelligence. If someday we meet a Mr. Spock or ET, or some other intelligent alien from another planet, this alien will have a right to life even if he isn't human.

But this is the limit of the common law's advancement. How intelligent does the creature need to be? Is the right to life connected to factors other than intelligence? How do we measure intelligence?

Should courts determine if there is a soul and if the right to life is connected to it? If so, how can a jury examine a soul to determine if and when it arrived or departed?

Animal rights activists say animals have a right to life. Well, which animals: chimpanzees, cats, mice, insects, fish? Where do we draw the line, and why there?

The whole topic of rights remains fuzzy, and so we have no guidelines for modern questions such as abortion, terminal illness, or euthanasia. I'm most concerned about abortion.

If an abortion is performed in the 36th week of a pregnancy, anyone would call this premeditated first degree murder. No one would object much if the mother and doctor were both sent to prison for a long, long time.

But suppose the abortion was performed in the first week? Should they go to prison then?

Where do we draw the line? Why there?

For miscarriages occurring in the first or second month, few people have funerals. Why?

Rights seem to be attached to intelligence. But we don't know what level of intelligence, or how to measure it. To be within the protection of the law, how smart is smart enough?

Suppose an adult suffers extensive brain damage from an illness or accident. Is euthanasia okay? Most would say no as long as any brain activity is detectable. To kill a person while the brain is operating even on a very low level is murder.

But an adult chimpanzee is more intelligent than a human infant. Is it murder to kill a chimpanzee?

To kill a dolphin? A dog?

How smart is smart enough?

A dog could easily be more intelligent than a brain-damaged human.

Where do we draw the line, and why there?

The question remains unanswered and we no longer have a trustworthy mechanism to answer it. All we have is political law—majority rule. If the majority of the voters or their representatives decide abortion in the first week is murder, it's murder. If they decide it isn't, it isn't. And if they change their minds, so be it. This is exactly what happened in Nazi Germany to Jews.

Chris, set the abortion question aside for a moment, we'll come back to it.

Originally in Germany the killing of any innocent human was held to be murder. Then political leaders acquired the power to change the law, and judges went along. Exceptions crept in. First it was persons held to be mentally incompetent. Then other "undesirables" became exceptions, until finally millions were killed. Legally.

In 1946, political law was exposed for the barbaric system it is.

At the Nuremberg trials the Nazi defendants claimed they were innocent of wrongdoing because they had been following orders.

They were within their nation's laws, this is true. But the prosecution argued that "there is a higher duty" than anything our governments can impose on us. The judges agreed: "The fact that the defendant acted pursuant to order of his government or of a superior shall not free him from responsibility." The defendants were executed.

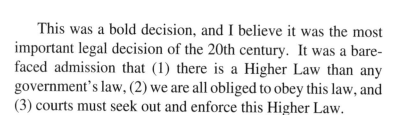

This was a bold decision, and I believe it was the most important legal decision of the 20th century. It was a bare-faced admission that (1) there is a Higher Law than any government's law, (2) we are all obliged to obey this law, and (3) courts must seek out and enforce this Higher Law.

Ever since, governments have done their best to bury the significance of the Nuremberg decision. They have largely succeeded. Today no one searches for Higher Law. Schools teach nothing about it. Few students know anything about Nuremberg.

This is why the abortion question is terrifying to me. The eventual resolution will very likely come through a constitutional amendment. And, pro or con, the answer will be important, but not half as important as the *method* of answering—through political means.

A right-to-life question will have been decided by majority rule. Could anything be more dangerous?

Once a right-to-life question has been decided democratically, then fourteen centuries of common law reasoning will be swept away. The right to life—your's, mine, and everyone else's—will be regarded not as a given, not as a gift from the Creator, but as a gift from the voters. And the voters can change their minds. The victory of political law will be complete. Nuremberg will be gone, and no one's life will be safe. Our legal system will be sitting squarely on the same foundations as that of Nazi Germany.

Chris, I hope you never forget either the Nuremberg decision or the terrible events that made the Nuremberg trials necessary. Millions were sent to the death camps because of the assumption that there was no law higher than the government's law.

Uncle Eric

22

Democracy and the Constitution

Dear Chris,

In 1978 a mass suicide occurred at Jonestown in Guyana. Nine-hundred Americans were told by their leader, Jim Jones, to kill themselves, and they did.

There's nothing new about mass lunacy. In the 1841 preface to EXTRAORDINARY POPULAR DELUSIONS AND THE MADNESS OF CROWDS, attorney Mackay wrote:

> Men, it has been well said, think in herds; it will be seen that they go mad in herds, while they only recover their senses slowly, and one by one.

Mackay's book is a long series of stories about such mass insanities as the Crusades, Tulipomania, The Mississippi Scheme, witch trials, and popular admiration of famous thieves.

In the ORIGINS OF TOTALITARIANISM, Hannah Arendt reminds us:

> Hitler's rise to power was legal in terms of majority rule and neither he nor Stalin could have maintained

the leadership of large populations, survived many interior and exterior crises, and braved numerous dangers of the relentless intra-party struggles if they had not had the confidence of the masses.

The great American financier Bernard Baruch said, "Anyone taken as an individual is tolerably sensible and reasonable—as a member of a crowd, he at once becomes a blockhead." Baruch earned millions by exploiting the crowd mentality of the investment markets.

I don't know the reason for this crowd mentality. Perhaps humans are pack animals. They seem to have an insatiable desire for leaders who will tell them how to think and act. Individualism is rare.

It's a mystery for psychologists and sociologists to solve. But America's Founders had to deal with it. As soon as the state governments became independent, these governments became more democratic, and more crazy.

They went wild printing money and caused a runaway inflation that led to a depression. The depression led to an armed uprising called Shay's Rebellion.

The state governments levied tariffs and other trade restrictions on citizens of neighboring states. Some officials even threatened war against neighboring states. Historians call this time of madness in America "The Critical Period." The blackjack mentality was running wild.

The Constitution and Federal Government were created as a control on the states. This was the Founders' way of stopping the democratic drift toward mob rule.

In other words, at the 1787 Constitutional Convention in Philadelphia *they were trying to thwart democracy to protect liberty.*

In fact, as far as I know, no one in the American Revolution was interested in democracy. Read the literature of 1776, try to find any mention of it. Everywhere you will find demands for liberty, but little or nothing about democracy. The Constitution says nothing about democracy.

The Founders did not like democracy and they did not trust it. They wanted liberty.

Indeed, as citizens of Britain, the early Americans probably already had more democracy than any other nation. To a large extent, this is what the war was about. The American colonists were a minority of the British population, which was governed by parliament's majority rule. Even if every one of the colonists could have voted, they probably could not have stopped parliament from voting against them. The Stamp Act, the Intolerable Acts, and other offensive legislation would have been enacted anyhow. If you are a member of a minority, living under majority rule just isn't all that great. Having your own representative in the legislature can be of some help, but if you can't persuade the majority to protect you, you're helpless.

The Founders studied the democracies of ancient Greece and other nations before they created the Constitution. In Federalist #10, James Madison wrote:

> Such democracies have ever been spectacles of turbulence and contention; have ever been found incompatible with personal security or the rights of property; and have in general been as short in their lives as they have been violent in their deaths.

In Federalist #50 he worried that,

> The passions, therefore, and not the reason, of the public would sit in judgment.

In speaking of the masses, Alexander Hamilton said:

Alexander Hamilton

> "The voice of the people has been said to be the voice of God; and, however generally this maxim has been quoted and believed, it is not true to fact. The people are turbulent and changing, they seldom judge or determine right."

Of all the Founders, Jefferson was probably the most trusting of the voters. But not even he would entertain for one minute the idea of unlimited majority rule. In an earlier letter I mentioned his remark,

It is strangely absurd to suppose that a million human
beings collected together are not under the same moral
rules as bind each of them separately.

Jefferson trusted farmers because of their work ethic, their
ownership of property, and their inability to form into large
crowds. As for those of us who aren't farmers:

The mobs of the great cities add just so much to the
support of pure government, as sores do to the strength
of the human body.

He was very much afraid that the government would
begin making exceptions to the principles that make liberty
possible:

A departure from principle in one instance becomes a
precedent for a second; that second for a third; and so
on, till the bulk of society is reduced to mere automa-
tons of misery, to have no sensibilities left but for
sinning and suffering.

Notice again the direct connection between liberty and
abundance. The Founders believed a nation that gives up its
liberty, automatically gives up its prosperity; millions slide
into poverty.

The decline might be gradual, even unnoticeable, but it
will happen. In 1776 they were not quite sure why this is, they
only knew it was. Today we know it's because of economic
calculation. The blackjack mentality stops progress.

What about compromise? Suppose, for instance, the
majority says to you, "Give us 50 percent of your money," and

you refuse. Should you relent when the majority returns and says, "Okay, we'll be reasonable, we'll settle for 25 percent." Jefferson said:

> Only lay down true principles, and adhere to them inflexibly.

The Founders' fear of democracy is apparent in the statistics of the times. Obstacles to voting were so extensive that less than three percent of the adult population were permitted to vote.[37] A person had to have light skin, a specified amount of property, specific religious beliefs, and be of the male gender.

Again, no one in 1776 was fighting for democracy, they were fighting for liberty, which is something entirely different. Liberty, requoting Jefferson, is "unobstructed action according to our will within limits drawn around us by the equal rights of others." Democracy, says Marshall Fritz, "is two wolves and a sheep voting to decide what's for lunch."

In Federalist Paper #48, James Madison wrote about democratically elected lawmakers:

> It will be no alleviation that these powers will be exercised by a plurality of hands, and not by a single one. One hundred and seventy-three despots would surely be as oppressive as one.

So why are we led to believe the Founders wanted America to be democratic?

---

[37] AMERICAN ACADEMIC ENCYCLOPEDIA, 1991, on Prodigy computerized data retrieval service.

They did include some minor elements of democracy in their new government. Three percent could vote. My guess is that this was a novelty in the world then—it still is in places—and voting is simple to understand. Common law is more complex. Apparently, writers focused on the novelty and jumped to the conclusion that this was the cause of America's wonderful liberty and abundance.

We should also note that a huge portion of the people were against creation of the Constitution and Federal Government altogether. Called anti-federalists, they were afraid the government would grow so large and voracious that eventually it would, in Patrick Henry's words, "oppress and ruin them." As leader of the anti-federalists, Henry said he "smelled a rat in Philadelphia."

Chris, in my next letter we'll get deeper into the Constitution. Until then, remember the early Americans wanted liberty, not democracy. The Founders were afraid of democracy, and to protect liberty they created the Constitution as a way to weaken democracy.

Uncle Eric

23

The Constitution:
Highest Law of the Land?

Dear Chris,

Here's a mystery. Article Six of the Constitution says:

This Constitution, and the laws of the United States
which shall be made in pursuance thereof; and all
treaties made, or which shall be made, under the
authority of the United States, shall be the supreme
law of the land; and the judges in every state shall be
bound thereby.

Supreme law of the land? This is a direct contradiction to
John Quincy Adams' remark I mentioned in an earlier letter:

Our political way of life is by the laws of nature, of
nature's God, and of course presupposes the existence
of God, the moral ruler of the universe, and a rule of
right and wrong, of just and unjust, binding upon man,
*preceding all institutions of human society and of
government.* [Emphasis added]

How can this be? Either Natural Law is the highest law or the Constitution is, it can't be both. As the saying goes, "No man can serve two masters."

We are not mind readers and cannot know exactly what the Founders were thinking when they wrote Article Six. But if we look at the conditions and beliefs of the times, we can make a good guess.

They knew the state democracies were degenerating into mob rule. They saw the Constitution as a control, a way to tame the state lawmakers. Many saw the Constitution as an emergency measure. They probably meant that it would be the highest human law.

This is supported by law professor Bruno Leoni in FREE-DOM AND THE LAW. Leoni points out that in the early 1800s legislation was seen mostly as only a rewrite of case law. The objective of statutes and constitutions alike was only to summarize and clarify common law, not overturn it.[38]

Also, we have the simple fact that the Founders weren't perfect. Maybe they became sloppy in their wording. In those days the existence of a Higher Law was taken for granted. Everyone knew about it, their ministers taught it to them. The Founders probably felt no need to phrase Article Six as carefully as we now know they should have. Certainly no one dreamed that the whole world would someday return to the arbitrary legal system of the Stone Age.

But maybe one man did. In a speech against the Constitution on June 14, 1788, Patrick Henry warned, "When our government was first instituted in Virginia, we declared the common law of England to be in force. That system of law

---

[38] p. 10.

which has been admired and has protected us and our ancestors is excluded [by the Constitution]. ... By this Constitution some of the best barriers of human rights are thrown away... That paper ought to have declared the common law in force."

Henry and his fellow anti-federalists were overruled and the Constitution was enacted without a clear protection for common law. If Madison and the other federalists were here today, I'm sure they'd be very sorry. They'd be doing all they could to correct their mistake.

Chris, in my next letter we'll talk more about the Constitution. Before we go on, I suggest you get a copy and read it. Don't read an interpretation, read a reprint of the original.

Uncle Eric

"But where, say some, is the king of America? I'll tell you friend, He reigns above, and does not make havoc of mankind like the royal brute of Britain. Yet, that we may not appear to be defective even in earthly honors, let a day be solemnly set apart for proclaiming the charter; let it be brought forth placed on the divine law, the word of God; let a crown be placed thereon, by which the world may know that so far as we approve of monarchy, that in America the law is king."

— Thomas Paine
COMMON SENSE, *January 1776*

24

Competing For Privilege

"No power on earth has a right to take our property from us without our consent."

— *John Jay*
ADDRESS TO THE PEOPLE OF BRITAIN
October 1774

Dear Chris,

Political law is not neutral, it is primarily a system for creating privileges. Much legislation is devoted to robbing Peter to subsidize Paul.

Not realizing a neutral form of law can exist, people today do not work to revive common law. They spend their energies competing to control the political law—competing for privilege. Everyone wants to be Paul and no one wants to be Peter.

So, we no longer have a concept of justice. We have only, "do unto others before they do it to you." Everyone is scrambling for control of the blackjack.

Having no legal system designed to search for eternal principles, courts seek to find ultimate law in the Constitution.

Do we have a right to freedom of expression? Some say yes, it's implied by the phrase "freedom of speech" in the First Amendment. Others say, no, "freedom of speech" means only that, speech. All assume law stops at the Constitution, there is nothing higher, no Higher Law, no higher principles.

The Constitution was never intended to be the answer to all questions. It was, mostly, just a set of guidelines for running the government—an owner's manual.

The Founders did their best to make it consistent with Natural Law.

Read it, examine the language. Notice rights are not granted by the Constitution, they are only protected by it. The Second Amendment, for instance, refers to "the right of the people"—it assumes the right already exists, and establishes a shield for it.

Those who believe the Constitution is the source of our rights should read the Ninth Amendment—it's only 21 words: "The enumeration in the Constitution, of certain rights, shall not be construed to deny or disparage others retained by the people."

Enumeration? Listing. Not granting, listing.

And other rights? Where do these others come from?

The Declaration of Independence tells us, "the Creator." How do we learn about them? Common law. Every legitimate legal principle goes back to the two originals taught by all religions and philosophies: Do all you have agreed to do, and do not encroach on other persons or their property.

When courts try to find ultimate law in the Constitution, they are looking in the wrong place. It's not there, and the Founders never intended to put it there. If the Founders knew how the Constitution is being used today, they'd laugh. Or cry.

Chris, in my next letter we'll begin learning about power. The Founders were deeply concerned, almost obsessed, about it, and we should be, too. Until then, remember that if you try to discover final answers in the Constitution you will fail. They aren't in there, and the Founders would be amazed that anyone would think they are.

Uncle Eric

Quotes from Thomas Jefferson

"The basis of our government being the opinion of the people, the very first object should be to keep that right; and were it left to me to decide whether we should have a government without newspapers, or newspapers without a government, I should not hesitate a moment to prefer the latter."

"I have sworn upon the altar of God, eternal hostility against every form of tyranny over the mind of man."

"If a nation expects to be ignorant and free, in a state of civilization, it expects what never was and never will be."

25

The Great Mystery

Dear Chris:

In an earlier letter I told you I'd be writing some things you might find surprising, maybe even unsettling. I suspect I've done that, but I'm not finished. I still have much more to tell you. All your life you've lived with only one side of this story about law, power, and government, and you deserve to hear the other.

In honesty, I should admit I'm uncomfortable doing this. My views on political power are identical to those of America's Founders, and I tend to write as passionately as they did. These views are so unusual in America today that they can be regarded as unpatriotic or subversive.

However, I am convinced you deserve to hear these views the way the Founders would want you to hear them, clear and unvarnished, so I will go ahead and write this way—their way. Just keep in mind that the country and the government are not the same thing, and I dearly love this country.

Let's continue.....

In the U.S. today there are two main political viewpoints, liberal and conservative. Liberals (the so-called left) believe in "social" freedom and economic control. They feel you should be able to read what you want, say what you want, and swallow what you want, but your production and trade should be tightly controlled by the government. They also believe your income should be taxed to whatever extent appears necessary to help the poor; and, the U.S. should stay out of foreign wars.

Conservatives (the right) are the reverse. They believe your production and trade should be free, and taxes very low, but the government should control licentious things like pornography, drugs, and gambling. They are also more willing to go to war.

These are simplifications, Chris, but for the purpose of these letters they will do. I will write to you more thoroughly about political philosophies in a future set of letters.[39]

We have a problem with this left versus right model. It doesn't tell us what liberals and conservatives will really do when they get into power. It explains only how liberals and conservatives think, not how they behave.

For example, conservatives want fewer taxes and they claim to work toward this goal. But each tax "reform" they give us seems to somehow yield a tax increase. This is a great mystery. Ronald Reagan was the most popular and powerful free-market president of the 20th century, but taxes at the end of his reign were higher than at the beginning. The Social Security "reform" of 1983 boosted taxes enormously.

And, while we are examining conservative behavior, since 1945 conservatives were very anti-Soviet. But in the

---

[39] Uncle Eric is referring to the Uncle Eric book ARE YOU LIBERAL? CONSERVATIVE? OR CONFUSED? by Richard J. Maybury, published by Bluestocking Press, web site: www.BluestockingPress.com, phone: 800-959-8586.

Iran-Iraq war (1980-88) they joined the Soviets in helping Iraq.

Worse, arch-conservative Ronald Reagan even helped pour U.S. money into the Soviet bloc. In 1981, at the exact time Mr. Reagan was making speeches about the "evil empire," the FEDERAL REGISTER published a declaration from President Reagan: "I determine that it is in the national interest for the Export-Import Bank of the United States to extend a credit in the amount of $120.7 million to the Socialist Republic of Romania." Romania was one of the most ruthless socialist states ever known.

The mystery involves liberals, too. Like the conservatives, they often behave opposite of what they think or say.

Liberals claim to be anti-war, but Franklin Roosevelt, the most liberal president of the 20th century, did a great deal to get the U.S. into World War II. He froze all Japanese assets, cut off the Japanese oil supply, and stopped Japanese access to iron and other vital raw materials.[40]

John Kennedy and Lyndon Johnson, two more liberal presidents, gave us the Vietnam War; Harry Truman the Korean War.

---

[40] This is not to imply that Japanese rulers were in any way innocent, they were barbarians. But Roosevelt picked a fight with them deliberately. He wanted into the war. If you have any doubts about this, first read ADMIRAL KIMMEL'S STORY by Admiral Husband E. Kimmel, then AND I WAS THERE by Admiral Edwin T. Layton. Layton was the intelligence officer at Pearl Harbor and Kimmel was the commander. Kimmel was railroaded into taking the blame for what Roosevelt and his cronies had done. In Kimmel's words, the soldiers and sailors who died at Pearl Harbor had unknowingly been used as a "lure for a Japanese attack." Also see WORLD WAR II: THE REST OF THE STORY AND HOW IT AFFECTS YOU TODAY by Richard J. Maybury, an Uncle Eric book, published by Bluestocking Press, phone: 800-959-8586, web site: www.BluestockingPress.com

Again, the way they think or the promises they make are often not the way they behave. So, if their beliefs are not a guide to their behavior, what is?

Political power. America's Founders believed it corrupts. No one can be trusted with it.

Our emphasis here is on political power, not power in general. As far as is known, humans are not corrupted by hydroelectric power, horsepower, economic power,[41] or solar power—just political power.

Here's my favorite remark about political power: "If once they [the people] become inattentive to the public affairs, you and I, and Congress and Assemblies, Judges and Governors, shall all become wolves."

This was written not by some small-time hack politician but by none other than Thomas Jefferson, one of the greatest political philosophers and statesmen in history. Jefferson knew how political power affects a person, and he knew that no human could be immune, not even himself. The blackjack can be seductive.

In my next letter we will look closely at political power. Exactly what is it? How does it affect a person's judgment?

For now, remember that the liberal vs. conservative or left vs. right political spectrum tells us how a person thinks, not how he will behave once he acquires political power.

Uncle Eric

---

[41] Economic power means wealth, and we have no evidence to indicate wealth corrupts. If it did, virtually every American would be corrupt because Americans are very wealthy compared to most of the rest of the world and to all of our ancestors. However, sometimes corrupt persons are able to acquire wealth. And wealthy persons are sometimes seduced by the temptations of political power and political privilege, which do corrupt.

26

The Privilege And The Thrill

"It will not be denied that power is of an encroaching nature."

— *James Madison*
Federalist Paper #48

Dear Chris,

So, what is political power?

Political power is the legal privilege of using force on persons who have not harmed anyone.

We all have the right to use force in self-defense, but political power is the use of force against the peaceful. The most common example is taxes. When officials collect taxes from John Q. Citizen they are saying, "Buy everything we are selling or men with guns will haul you away to prison."

John Q. Citizen hasn't done anything to harm anyone, but he is being threatened with force. Government is the only institution permitted to do this. No church, charity, business, or other private organization can force John to purchase its goods or services, or force him to obey its commands—he can always walk away.

In one way or another, most of the government's laws are backed by force—by the blackjack.

A political powerseeker is a person who wants the legal privilege of using guns, chains, and prisons to make you do as he thinks you should. He may not admit it, he may not even fully understand it, but, the bottom line is, a political powerseeker desires the legal privilege of using force to get what he wants—although he probably does have good intentions. Founder John Adams referred to "cruel power;" his colleague, John Dickinson, referred to "brutal power."

> *"The glory of great men should always be measured by the means they have used to acquire it."*
>
> —*La Rochefoucauld*
> *"Quotable Quotes"*
> READERS DIGEST
> *September, 1991*

It's evil. One of the age-old problems with political power is that a person who will accept it cannot be trusted with it.

In his First Inaugural Address in 1801, Jefferson nailed down the problem with his usual razor-sharp logic:

> Sometimes it is said that man cannot be trusted with the government of himself. Can he, then, be trusted with the government of others?

Political power is not a skill or a talent. It is not the ability to manipulate objects or create wealth. It is not the capacity to build a better world. It is force used on human beings. It is something done *to* someone.

Usually the force is carefully disguised, but it's there in the background waiting to be used if you do not obey—the mailed fist in the velvet glove.

Chris, at this point I want to caution you to use every effort to think with your mind and not your heart. If you are uncomfortable with this letter, it might be because your emotional patriotism for your country is sending you a confused message. In an earlier letter I said that America is a country that was founded on principle, not on geography. I suspect your discomfort comes from your confusion on this point. Through the years you may have unconsciously absorbed the emotional message, "my country right or wrong." Right now, you might be feeling like a she-bear who's ready to defend her cub from any possible threat. You might be ready to lash out at anyone or anything that seems to threaten your beloved America. Yes, I am critical of politics. But remember, politics is not America. The America I love is the America of principle, not of geography and not of politics. So, for our purposes here, please rein in your emotions so your reasoning mind can race ahead. Let's continue....

Do not confuse political power with influence. Corporations and other private organizations can exert influence, especially monetary influence, but they cannot use guns, chains, or prisons. Governments can come to your home and drag you off to jail.

Those who argue that the difference between influence and power is slight have never been shot. Political power is violence. As dictator Mao Tse-Tung admitted, "Political power grows out of the barrel of a gun."

For analyzing investment and economic trends, I've found some of the best insights about political power in the book I mentioned in a previous letter, THE IDEOLOGICAL ORIGINS OF THE AMERICAN REVOLUTION by historian Bernard Bailyn. The leaders of the American Revolution did more scholarly work on the nature of power than anyone before or since, and Bailyn gives a good summary of this work.

Most revealing is Samuel Adams' remark about the "lust of power," which Adams said is one of the "predominant passions" of human beings.

Their study of history led the Founders to the conclusion that the attractions of political power are not so much intellectual as physiological. This is important. Quoting the early Americans, historian Bailyn tells us power "is known to be intoxicating," and "intoxicating and liable to abuse." It "converts a good man in private life to a tyrant in office." Power causes "wantonness."

None of the Founders' beliefs about political power would come as a surprise to one who has worked in the offices of congresspersons or other top officials. The extent of the lying, back-stabbing, womanizing, drunkenness, and general debauchery at the higher levels of governments is extraordinary and has been since the days of the Roman orgies. In 1770, William Pitt, a politician with long experience at the top levels of government, observed that power "is apt to corrupt the minds of those who possess it."

Chris, you haven't studied these ideas in your history, civics, or government classes. I'm giving you the other side of the story so you can use your good mind to draw your own conclusions.

My own theory is that political power has an addictive, drug-like effect on humans because of our biological ancestry. Visit a history museum and you will see skeletons of huge animals that are extinct now but roamed the earth only a few thousand years ago. The mammoths and sabre-toothed tigers are awesome.[42]

Surviving in that world, armed only with spears and clubs, must have been a mighty challenge. Our ancestors had

---

[42] These animals should not be confused with dinosaurs which scientists estimate being millions of years old. Mammoths and sabre-toothed tigers were recent, perhaps as little as 5000 years old. In 1799, arctic explorers found complete mammoths frozen in ice in Siberia. The meat was still fresh enough to be used as food for sled dogs.

to have some kind of edge, some kind of biochemical booster that enabled a 150-pound man to attack and kill his 2000-pound adversaries.

I believe it is this booster that is triggered when political power is used. A politician feels the "rush" that our primitive ancestors felt when they went up against the mammoth. He gets charged up and eventually becomes addicted to this high.

When a child ties a tin can to a dog's tail, is this an early manifestation of political power? Does the child get the same sort of "rush"?

When a school bully intimidates a classmate, is this political power?

When a street gang dominates its turf, is this political power?

And when a majority votes to tax a minority, is this political power?

In his 1776 pamphlet COMMON SENSE, Thomas Paine referred to the "thirst for arbitrary power." At the end of this letter, I'll include some additional thoughts about political power for you to think about—written by individuals as diverse as Plato, Hitler, and Emerson.

Based on my own study and observation it seems that once a powerseeker has been into his addiction for a few months he begins to lose his moral sense. He becomes not immoral but amoral, he'll say or do anything necessary to feel the rush. He's a junkie.

Most interesting is the similarity of the rush produced by political power to that produced by cocaine. Medical reports describe the cocaine rush as an "increase of heart and breathing rates" accompanied by a feeling of "stimulation, exhilaration" and "limitless power."[43]

---

[43] THE INFORMATION PLEASE ALMANAC, p. 102

One of the latest theories about drug addiction suggests that drugs produce pleasant feelings because they are artificial substitutes for body chemicals that do this naturally.

Could cocaine be an artificial substitute for body chemicals activated by political power?

As I said, most of the best research on political power was done two centuries ago by America's Founders, long before the science of biochemistry existed. I wonder what we'd learn today using modern scientific techniques.

A small amount of work along these lines has been done. The book PSYCHOPOLITICAL ANALYSIS edited by Elizabeth Wirth Marvick is a collection of the research done by psychologist Nathan Leites.

Much of Leites' attention is focused on the "collapse of ethical feelings" experienced by powerseekers. While investigating Russian politics, Leites came across interesting comments in Russian literature: "There are some people who have an urge to do the dirty even on their closest friends and very often without any good reason for it." And, "Our historical pastime is the direct satisfaction of inflicting pain." One Russian writer said, "It is sometimes very pleasant to smash things."

Chris, in the next letter we'll continue learning about power. Remember that political power is the privilege of using force—the blackjack—on persons who have not harmed anyone. This is what sets government apart from all charities, businesses, and other institutions.

Uncle Eric

Peace Officer or Police Officer?

Why is it that we all like peace officers, but many of us are afraid of police officers and all are terrified of a police state?

What's the difference between a peace officer and a police officer?

Look in a dictionary. The word police comes from the same Latin root as politics. A police officer enforces the laws of the state.

A peace officer keeps the peace. He enforces the two fundamental laws that make civilization possible. He fights encroachment and fraud. He protects us.

A police officer does whatever politicians tell him, even if this means breaking the peace and encroaching on others.

In short, countries that are free have peace officers, and countries that are unfree have police officers.

Thoughts About Political Power

"Power is pleasure.   — William Hazlitt, 1826

"The pleasure of governing must certainly be exquisite, if we may judge from the vast numbers who are eager to be concerned with it."
                    — Voltaire, 1764

"Our power placed us above the rest."
                    — Winston Churchill, 1943

"The wise become as the unwise in the enchanted chambers of power."
                    — Walter Savage Landor, 1853

"Power, like a desolating pestilence, pollutes whatever it touches."
                    — Percy Bysshe Shelley, 1813

"You shall have joy, or you shall have power, said God, you shall not have both."
                    — Ralph Waldo Emerson, 1842

"There is a possible Nero in the gentlest human creature that walks."
                    — Thomas Bailey Aldrich, 1903

"Our sense of power is more vivid when we break a man's spirit than when we win his heart."
                    — Eric Hoffer, 1954

"Power-worship blurs political judgment because it leads, almost unavoidably, to the belief that present trends will continue. Whoever is winning at the moment will always seem to be invincible."
— George Orwell, 1950

"The one means that wins the easiest victory over reason: terror and force." — Adolph Hitler, 1924

"When the tyrant has disposed of foreign enemies by conquest or treaty, and there is nothing to fear from them, then he is always stirring up some war or other, in order that the people may require a leader."
— Plato, 347 B.C.

"Politics, as a practice, whatever its professions, has always been the systematic organization of hatreds." — Henry Adams, 1907

"It is said that 'power corrupts,' but actually it's more true that power attracts the corruptible. The sane are usually attracted by other things than power."
— David Brin, 1985

"Even a casual scrutiny of history reveals that we humans have a sad tendency to make the same mistakes again and again. Having power tends to corrupt us."
— Carl Sagan and Ann Druyan
"Real Patriots Ask Questions"
PARADE MAGAZINE, September 8, 1991

27

The Fun Is In The Playing

Dear Chris,

In this letter I'll continue giving you the other side of the story about law, power, and government.

Social activists observe our chronic unemployment and poverty, and they complain about the "abuse of power" they feel is the cause. They miss the point. Power cannot be abused, power is abuse. These hardships are its natural offspring.

In THE FEDERALIST PAPERS, James Madison and Alexander Hamilton were very clear about their belief that political power corrupts large groups and majorities as easily as it corrupts individuals. Madison wrote that "the majority," having "a passion or interest, must be rendered...unable to concert and carry into effect schemes of oppression."

As mentioned in an earlier letter, history is rife with examples where the majority was corrupted by its power: the French Reign of Terror, the Salem witch trials, Nazi Germany, the Inquisition, slavery, Chairman Mao's Cultural Revolution.

In a 1775 letter to her husband, John Adams, Abigail Adams wrote:

I am more and more convinced that man is a dangerous creature and that power, whether vested in many or a few, is ever grasping, and, like the grave, cries "Give, give."

Part of the problem is that the total I.Q. of a group of people goes down as the group grows larger. But more important is the sheer thrill of exerting power, of domination, of conquest. The biochemical high. A mob demanding a new law or a new war is feeling the same rush as a band of cavemen spearing the mammoth.

I'm reminded of the cartoon in which a club-wielding member of a lynch mob asks a companion, "This guy we're going after, what did he do?"

The only solution is the one America's Founders tried to implement: (1) Have as little government as possible so that whoever gets control of it will not be able to do much damage, and (2) for production of essential goods and services use private organizations that cannot back their decisions with force.

This is what the 1787 Constitutional Convention and 1790 Bill of Rights were all about. The Founders were trying to keep government small and weak so that persons with good intentions would not be able to get control and send us down the road to hell. They were trying to nail the blackjack to the floor.

But for our discussion in this letter, the most important point is that political power is like alcohol or any other drug. It causes a person to behave in ways that are predictable.

If someone tells you they have a spouse who is an alcoholic, you instantly have a rather clear picture of their home life and job performance. Alcohol corrupts humans in ways that are predictable. The same for PCP or heroin. Each drug produces a characteristic set of behaviors. And so does political power.

This is why anti-tax conservatives bring us higher taxes and anti-war liberals get us into wars. They are controlled not by their beliefs but by their addictions.

The most prominent characteristic they share with other addicts is deceitfulness, they can't be trusted. They say what they must to get what they want.

As for their interest in war, the best analogy I've been able to come up with is chess. Being a chess player, Chris, you know that most of the fun is in the playing, not the winning. You will play even when you know you are sure to lose because the satisfaction comes from the game itself. Victory is secondary.

Powerseekers enact laws, collect taxes, and get us into wars for the same reason. The thrill of power comes from the use of the power; the end result isn't all that important to them. They will get us into a war even if they know we will lose because playing and losing is preferable to not playing at all.

How else explain the 1983 Lebanon debacle? As I write this today, we still don't know why the Marines were sent in, why they were placed in such a dangerous area, or why they were misinformed about their neutrality. All we know is that the U.S. entered the war in Lebanon and lost—just like Vietnam.

Playing and losing is better than not playing at all. Neither Jefferson nor Madison would have been surprised about Lebanon or Vietnam. They'd be surprised only that we were surprised.

John Adams warned that groups of politicians can be subject to "fits of humor, starts of passion, flights of enthusiasm, partialities, or prejudice, and consequently productive of hasty results and absurd judgments." Political power corrupts the mind. Humans are not made to be gods, they can't handle it.

Psychologist Leites writes that a politician often feels that "I may act without any regard for the predictability of the outcome or for the success of the collective operation in which I participate."

This is why I want to emphasize that I don't believe politicians can help it. They are addicts. In the intellectual sense, they don't like insane laws, taxes, or wars any more than you or I do, but they get into these because it's the only way to feel the thrill. Heroin addicts don't like needles, but they use them.

Politicians tell themselves they are doing it for us, but they are really doing it to us. This is the source of their rush. They won't admit it, not even to themselves, but doing things *to* people is what gives them pleasure. And, I'm not sure they should be blamed. In our culture today political power is regarded as good. We are all taught that everyone should have it and use it.

Political powerseekers have three priorities:

> Top priority: To keep the power they have.
>
> Second priority: To use it on someone—to feel the thrill of spearing the mammoth.
>
> Third priority: To get more power.

These goals might sound similar to those of corporate presidents or other heads of private organizations. The difference is that heads of private organizations cannot use guns, chains, and prisons on us.

Notice that these priorities have nothing to do with money. *Politicians are a different breed than the rest of us, they are not seekers of profit.* For most of them, money is not a reward, it is only a tool that is sometimes useful in gaining and using power. I remember watching one California politician spend more than a million dollars of his own money to gain an office that paid only a few thousand per year.

> The only prize much cared for by the powerful is power.
>
> — Oliver Wendell Holmes, Jr., 1913

When an important issue arises and you are trying to discover how the lawmakers will respond to it, place yourself in their shoes. Ask yourself, "If I were they and had their priorities, what would I do?" My personal estimate is that you will predict correctly at least 80 percent of the time.

Granted, this system isn't infallible, but it works better than any other I know of. Learn all you can about political power and its economic effects. The best places to start are THE FEDERALIST PAPERS by Madison, Hamilton, and Jay, and a book called THE LIFE AND SELECTED WRITINGS OF THOMAS JEFFERSON edited by Adrienne Koch and William Peden.

Before moving on to the next letter I'd like to clear up a possible misunderstanding. Someone might read these letters and jump to the conclusion that I believe a vast conspiracy is behind it all. I don't. I do believe conspiracies exist and the conspirators are trying to steer events in directions favorable to them. But these conspiracies are not the root of the problem. The root is political power. Eliminate all the conspirators without eliminating these gigantic governments they are trying to control and two weeks later we'd just have a whole new crop of conspirators trying to gain control of the governments.

They'd have little choice. No wealthy person can afford to be without connections in the government when the government has the power to take everything he has.

In short, conspiracies exist and they bear watching, but they are symptoms, not causes. The cause is political power. It corrupts.

Chris, what do you think so far? The hope of the future rests with people who, like the American Founders, recognize that power is brutality and are suspect of crowds. But these people are, unfortunately, rare. Few have heard the other side of the story, which is why I write these letters. We must spread the word.

Uncle Eric

Abigail Adams
Painting by
Gilbert Stuart
Reproduced from the
DICTIONARY OF
AMERICAN PORTRAITS,
published by Dover
Publications, Inc.
1967

"I am more and more convinced that man is a dangerous creature and that power, whether vested in many or a few, is ever grasping, and, like the grave, cries 'Give, give.' "

—Abigail Adams

28

The Lessons of Simon Bolivar

Dear Chris,

We can learn important lessons by examining the exploits of Simon Bolivar in our neighboring countries in South America. These countries all have democracy—sometimes.

Born in 1783, Bolivar was well-educated. He was impressed by the American Revolution and the new philosophy of freedom that was spreading around the world.

A great admirer of the American Founders, Bolivar launched a revolution in Latin America to copy them, to free South America from Spain. It was one of the most successful revolutions in history. Bolivar freed not one country but six: Venezuela, Columbia, Ecuador, Panama, Peru, and Bolivia (which was named after him).

But after the revolution Bolivar was faced with the same problem every other revolutionary faces. Now that the old political system was gone, what could he create to replace it?

There are two general models of how political change unfolds, the American Revolution and the French Revolution. The symbol of the American Revolution is the Liberty Bell. The symbol of the French Revolution is the guillotine.

The American Revolution was based on the principles of the old British common law. The French Revolution was based on democracy, majority rule.

The American Revolution led to the most free and prosperous nation ever known. The French Revolution led to the Reign of Terror and the Napoleonic Wars.

Bolivar was faced with the same problem encountered by the people of East Europe and the Soviet Union in 1990 when the Soviet Empire began disintegrating. Being of non-British origins, they had no background in British common law.

Bolivar's revolution led not to liberty but to democracy and war, the French model. After separating from Spain, Chile went to war against Peru and Bolivia, Paraguay against Argentina, and assassinations and uprisings became the national sports of Latin America.

In 1828, in an attempt to bring stability, Bolivar, the great champion of liberty, became a dictator.

But he failed to copy the American Founders' success. In the latin nations nothing worked then and nothing works today. The latin nations still ride a pendulum that swings every few years from dictatorship to democracy and chaos, then back to dictatorship, and so on.

Genuine liberty is not possible for them because these nations never adopted a rational legal system. Their people have never known about Natural Law, common law, the two fundamental laws, or free markets. They know only democracy, majority rule. Some have had dozens of revolutions in which the streets have been paved with bodies.

Because they have no legal stability, these countries are unsafe for investment. Anyone who is smart enough to earn extra money is smart enough to send it out of the country to Switzerland or some other safe haven beyond the reach of the next dictator.

Without this money, factories and other job-creating businesses are not built. Poverty in Latin America is never ending.

The latin nations are economic disaster areas eclipsed only by the African nations, which have exactly the same problem, political law. Their legal systems enforce majority rule or dictatorial rule, not Higher Law.

I once met an American investor who had thought it was safe to get involved in a business venture in a newly democratic nation. He lost a fortune but didn't understand why until he heard one of my speeches about common law. If you know anyone who is headed into this same mistake, you might want to let him read these letters.

Chris, if you want to understand what is happening in your world today, study the differences between the French Revolution and the American Revolution. The French went after democracy; the Americans went after liberty. The French got mob rule and the Reign of Terror; the Americans got the most free and prosperous nation ever seen on earth.

As you watch events unfold in other nations, remember Simon Bolivar. History repeats.

Uncle Eric

29

Eating The Seed Corn
Causing Unemployment and Poverty

Dear Chris,

Why does America, the land of opportunity, now have so much unemployment and poverty? And why does so much of this unemployment and poverty seem to be permanent? One reason is a shortage of seed corn.

When farmers grow crops, they do not eat or sell the whole crop. Some is kept back, saved, to be used as seed for next year's crop. This savings is called seed corn. An abundance of food is possible only if someone is saving large quantities of seed corn.

In other parts of the economy, seed corn takes the form of saving money. The savings are placed into stocks, bonds, and other investments where they are used to build factories, offices, and other places of work. These places of work are the source of jobs and incomes. In every nation, they are the most important force in eliminating poverty.

To have an abundance of good jobs and incomes, a nation must have an abundance of savings, an abundance of "seed corn."

When a government grows so large that the taxpayers become angry at the high taxes, the government sometimes tries to delay collection of the taxes by borrowing. This borrowing diverts the flow of money away from the investments that create the jobs and incomes. It causes a shortage of these investments, which means a shortage of the jobs and incomes.

This is called "crowding out." The government crowds businesses and employees out of the economy, thereby creating unemployment and poverty. In other words, the government eats our seed corn.

Do not fall into the trap of thinking of unemployment and poverty as statistics or percentages. A six percent unemployment rate means millions of fine, innocent people are suffering in uncountable ways. Stress, hardship, bankruptcy, alcoholism, drug abuse, divorce, juvenile delinquency — the list of agonies goes on and on. Desperation.

A nation that has a shortage of seed corn has an appointment with disaster.

Uncle Eric

To pay for its spending the Federal Government is, at the time I write this, borrowing money at the rate of $1.0 million every two minutes.

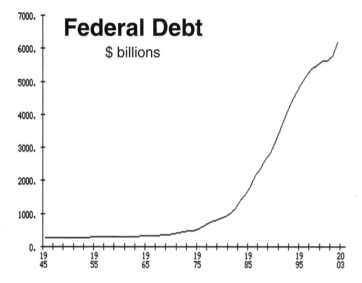

> "*Even if federal deficits could be reduced to a 'mere' $100 billion annually, the compounding of national debt and interest payments by the early twenty-first century will still cause quite unprecedented totals of money to be diverted in that direction. Historically, the only other example which comes to mind of a Great Power so increasing its indebtedness in peacetime is France in the 1780s, where the fiscal crisis contributed to the domestic political crisis.*"

— Paul Kennedy
THE RISE AND FALL OF THE GREAT POWERS, 1987

The French Revolution began in 1789 and led to the Reign of Terror and the Napoleonic Wars.

30

Origin of Government

"The sheep are happier of themselves, than under the care of wolves."

— *Thomas Jefferson*

Dear Chris,

When you are finished with this letter I doubt you'll ever see the world the same again. Furthermore, you will know things that some people don't want you to know. This side of the story may make you uncomfortable because it's so different from anything you've heard before. Keep in mind that America is a wonderful country, but the country and the government are not the same thing. You are old enough now to hear the other side.

Jefferson believed it imperative that individuals be correctly informed. He said:

I know no safe depository of the ultimate powers of the society but the people themselves; and if we think them not enlightened enough to exercise their control with a wholesome discretion, the remedy is not to take it from them but to inform their discretion.

When living in a government-controlled economy as we do today, you will be better able to manage your career and investments if you understand the nature and behavior of government. Obvious, right? If you try to make decisions based on fictions, you'll be running much risk.

So, what is the real nature and behavior of government? Where did government come from?

Any child knows the answers, right? It's easy. The institution of government was invented long, long ago to help us. People needed certain essential services, especially law enforcement, so they got together, chose someone to be their government, and voluntarily agreed to pay taxes for the services the government would provide.

This is the official story we are all taught. It sounds good except for two small problems. First, no historian has ever been able to find an example of this happening. In A THEORY OF THE ORIGIN OF THE STATE, anthropologist Robert L. Carneiro writes, "We now know that no such compact was ever subscribed to by human groups."[44] Sociologist Franz Oppenheimer, writing in THE STATE, is more blunt. He calls this explanation "a fairy tale"[45] and is distressed that it is "prevalent in university teaching."[46]

The second problem with the official story is, as economist Murray Rothbard notes in FOR A NEW LIBERTY, "By far the overwhelming portion of all enslavement and murder in the history of the world have come from the hands of government." This is an institution designed to help us?

---

[44] A THEORY OF THE ORIGIN OF THE STATE by Robert L. Carneiro, Institute for Humane Studies, George Mason University, VA, p. 4.

[45] THE STATE by Franz Oppenheimer, Viking Press, Free Life Editions, New York, 1944, p. 5.

[46] Ibid. p. 4.

The official explanation for the origin of government is quite wrong and dangerously misleading. It creates a false sense of security, and none of America's Founders would want us to believe it. I will give you a few of their remarks shortly.

The official explanation actually applies more to the origin of common law than to government.

Carneiro and Oppenheimer explain, in a much more scholarly fashion than I will here, the real reason government was invented.

Historians and anthropologists have now located many examples of peaceful communities that had gangs of barbarians living nearby. Imagine one of our more violent gangs riding into town on horses, instead of motorcycles or cars, and you will have the picture.

These barbarians were lazy and had little interest in work. Every few weeks they would ride into town, steal food, clothing, and whatever else they could carry, then ride back out. They would live off this stolen loot until it was gone, then ride back in and raid the town again.

This would go on for many years until—

One night, as the barbarians were sitting around their campfire planning their next attack, one complained, "You know, all this riding in and out of town fighting with people is beginning to feel like work. It isn't fun anymore, there's got to be a better way."

Another lamented, "You're right, in the last raid I lost an ear and two more fingers. I'm running out of parts."

This sorrowful discussion would continue until someone exclaimed, "I've got it! Let's just ride into town and stay! We'll put up a building in the middle of town and call it City Hall or State Capitol or some such thing, and we'll use it as a hangout. We'll take baths and shave and dress up in fine clothes like respectable businessmen. Then we'll levy something we'll call a tax.

"We'll tell the people—we'll call them taxpayers—that as long as they pay this tax regularly, exactly as we tell them, with the right forms and everything, we won't punish them. We'll start the tax low so that they won't feel it's worth fighting over, and each year we'll raise it a bit until we're taking a sizable part of their incomes."

Another barbarian suggested, "Yes, and we could use some of the tax money to provide a few services, maybe streets, schools, and courts, so that the people will feel they're getting something for their money."

And another added the final touches. "There are other gangs in this area. When they see how docile our taxpayers have become, they'll try to ride in and take over. They'll be shearing our sheep. We'll need to provide police and an army to protect what's ours. The taxpayers will love it—they'll think we're doing it for them."

Carneiro says this was the essential process for the invention of governments in "Mesopotamia, Egypt, India, China, Japan, Greece, Rome, northern Europe, central Africa, Polynesia, Middle America, Peru, and Columbia, to name only the most prominent examples."[47] Oppenheimer adds Britain, France, Arabia, Italy, Germany, Spain, Mexico, and many others.[48] All governments today have evolved from these origins.

In other words, governments do not collect taxes to provide services, they provide services as an excuse to collect taxes. A tax is a substitute for a raid.

---

[47] Ibid. p. 6.
[48] Ibid. p. 8.

You might remember in my first letter that I said the country and the government are not the same thing. Now you know why. The government is a group of politicians and bureaucrats who are gradually conquering the country.

Have you ever heard this side of the story before? It is rather startling, isn't it? And it explains why governments have been wrecking economies, creating poverty, and murdering and enslaving people for thousands of years. It's what they were invented to do. It's the nature of the beast.

It's also why America's Founders were convinced political power corrupts. John Adams said, "Fear is the foundation of most governments," and Thomas Paine asked, "From such beginnings of governments, what could be expected, but a continual system of war and extortion?"

Carneiro observes: "A close examination of history indicates that only a coercive theory can account for the rise of the state."[49]

Oppenheimer said: "Everywhere, we find some warlike tribe of wild men breaking through the boundaries of some less warlike people, settling down as nobility and founding its State."[50]

Remember the barbarians who took over Europe after the Roman Empire fell? The feudal kingdoms?

When you visit Europe and England you will see a castle every few miles. Probably the most famous are the castles on the Rhine.

The Romans had owned plantations called latifundia. A gang of barbarians would overrun a latifundium, force the workers into a kind of slavery called serfdom, and make these serfs build them a fort called a castle. The gang would set up

---

[49] Ibid. p. 6.
[50] Ibid. p. 8.

housekeeping in the castle and live off the taxes they collected from the serfs.

This is royalty. We are led to believe kings and queens are like movie stars, glamorous and wealthy. Children are told stories in which the young heroine dreams of becoming a princess and marrying a handsome young prince.

Marrying a handsome young prince meant marrying a handsome young gangster, and, in some cases, a handsome young mass murderer.

Granted, royalty means wealth, but the wealth came through conquest. It was stolen, not earned. A castle was not so much a romantic palace as a plush headquarters of a concentration camp. When you visit one, ask to see not just the stately halls and bedrooms, but the dungeons and torture chambers, too.

Royalty means bullying and tyranny. Far from being "highness," these people were the lowest, they were preda-tors. Today's royalty are descended from them. In many cases, their enormous wealth is loot their ancestors stole. Their prestige is from the time when they had their victims convinced kings had a special divine right to prey on others.

It's difficult for us today to imagine how brutal and corrupt royalty was. In Europe their political law said a young bride could not sleep with her groom until she first allowed herself to be raped by the king.

America's Founders hated royalty. This is not an exag-geration. They felt contempt, revulsion.

When Jefferson was U.S. minister to France, he was amazed at the degeneracy of the royalty. He wrote that Gustavus III of Sweden and Joseph II of Austria were crazy; Charles IV of Spain and Ferdinand IV of Naples were fools; Maria, queen of Portugal, was an idiot, and Frederick William II of Prussia was "a mere hog in body as well as mind." He referred to all royalty as "animals" who had "become without mind."[51]

Is this someone you'd want your daughter to marry?

This is not a small point. These fantasies about handsome princes and beautiful princesses are dangerous; they whitewash the truth. They give children the impression political power is wonderful stuff.

A castle was a hangout for silk-clad gangsters who were stealing from helpless workers. The king was the "lord" who had control of the blackjack; he claimed a special "divine right" to use force on the innocent.

The British government evolved from these feudal origins, and the U.S. Government from the British government.

The world's early governments evolved into those we have today and all have retained their essential natures. To get what they want, they use force. The force is usually hidden but it's there, and you will feel it if you resist.

I believe a major reason America and the world have gotten into so much trouble during the 20th and 21st centuries

Castles were not beautiful palaces for heroic princes and princesses. Most were headquarters for concentration camps. These camps, called feudal kingdoms, were established by conquering barbarians who had enslaved the local people. Fairy tales about castles and royalty give impressionable young minds the idea that political power is good.

---

[51] Letter to J. Langdon, 1810.

is that we have forgotten that, fundamentally, governments are predators. Attempts to make them do good are attempts to make the leopard change his spots. Maybe it can be done, but 6000 years of history are not encouraging.

My experience has been that deep in their hearts most people sense there is something inherently wrong with government. Is there any country where the word politics is not pronounced with a sneer? But while they were still children, they were taught that political power is brilliant, beautiful, noble, and desirable. Cinderella. Prince Valiant.

But government is good, isn't it? Bureaucracies exist to solve problems for us, don't they?

In A TIME FOR ACTION, former U.S. Treasury Secretary William Simon writes:

> The bureaucrat's first objective, of course, is preservation of his job—provided by the big-government system, at taxpayer's expense. ... Whether real-world problems get solved or not is of secondary importance. It doesn't take much cynicism, in fact, to see that the bureaucrats have a vested interest in not having problems solved. If the problems did not exist (or had not been invented), there would be no reason for the bureaucrat to have a job.

Notice Simon's remark, "had not been invented." Remember my earlier group of letters about inflation, recessions, unemployment, and poverty?[52]

---

[52] See WHATEVER HAPPENED TO PENNY CANDY? by Richard J. Maybury, published by Bluestocking Press, phone: 800-959-8586, web site: www.BluestockingPress.com

After he had been president, Jefferson sent a letter to Scottish geographer John Melish dated January 13, 1813. In this letter Jefferson made an interesting statement: "An honest man can feel no pleasure in the exercise of power over his fellow citizens."

> *"This and no other is the root from which a tyrant springs; when he first appears he is a protector."*
> — *Plato*
> *circa 400 B.C.*

Think about this. An honest man will not like political power. What does this tell us about the inherent nature of government?

You've probably read statements by politicians complaining that no matter how hard they try to do good, it never comes out the way they plan. Sometimes they even feel compelled to do what they know isn't right.

They probably do not realize it, but this is because they are part of an institution that is designed to use force—to do damage. Good intentions matter little.

The most difficult lesson every social activist eventually learns is that if you wait for the government to solve your problems, you'll wait for a very long time.

Chris, as I mentioned in an earlier letter, most people today think law and government are the same thing. The reason is that in every society I know of, the first industry the government nationalizes[53] is the justice industry. Law contains the guidelines for the use of force, and governments want control of these guidelines so that they can make themselves exempt.

Now that you've heard the other side of the story about law, power, and government, what do you think of it?

---

[53] Nationalization means the government taking ownership.

Before I close this letter, let me emphasize that I am not accusing government bureaucrats of intentionally doing anything wrong. They haven't heard the other side of the story either — as children, they heard the same fairy tales you and I did — and I'm sure most believe the benefits of what they do are greater than the costs. Many costs are hidden.

Until next time, remember that law and government are two very different institutions. Indeed, they are opposites. Governments and their legislation are the natural enemies of real law. They were invented for the purpose of encroachment. George Washington:

"Government is not reason; it is not eloquence; it is force. Like fire, it is a dangerous servant and a fearful master."

Uncle Eric

"It sounds a little grand, I know, to say my lawyers in the plural, but I didn't start out that way. I started with one lawyer, but you know what happens. One moves in and pretty soon there are seven, all in the same office. They get together all day long and say to each other, 'What can we postpone next?' The only thing they don't postpone, of course, is their bill, which arrives regularly. You've heard about the man who got the bill from his lawyer which said, 'For crossing the street to speak to you and discovering it was not you...twelve dollars.' "

— George S. Kaufman's biography
quoted in the WALL STREET JOURNAL

31

Are Lawyers and Judges Corrupt?

"As the American Bar Association convenes its annual meeting this week in Atlanta, the esteem of its members stands at an all-time low. The profession is under attack from all sides. ... Lawyer jokes are getting abrasive."

— *THE ECONOMIST MAGAZINE*[54]

Dear Chris,

Judges are lawyers, and lawyers are no longer respected as they once were. When I was young I'd occasionally hear a snide remark or wisecrack about lawyers. Now it's outright ridicule, sometimes hatred.

This should not be surprising. How can lawyers be respected when the law itself is corrupt?

The public knows something is wrong, and they direct their frustrations at the lawyers. I do not think they are aware of how many lawyers have been trying to draw attention to the corruption of the law.

In my second letter I mentioned Judge Clarence Thomas' belief in Natural Law and his speech referring to John Quincy Adams. Judge Thomas is not alone.

---

[54] THE ECONOMIST MAGAZINE, August 10, 1991.

Charles Meachling, Jr. is an international lawyer, former Cambridge law professor, and U.S. State Department official. In the BROOKINGS REVIEW he wrote:

In the U.S. the sanctimonious maxim that "Ignorance of the law is no excuse" puts every citizen at risk. That may have been a sound rule in simpler times, when the catalog of punishable offenses was limited to traditional offenses like murder, robbery, rape, and larceny, but it becomes a sinister joke when applied to the five-foot shelf of the U.S. criminal code and the even more voluminous statutes of individual states.

Moreover, in the U.S. a citizen cannot rely on the plain meaning of a statute, or what passes for it. He must retain a lawyer to parse its legislative history and judicial evolution. So many forms of social and economic activity have now been criminalized that the discretionary power of federal and state authorities to pick and choose targets for prosecution has made enforcement utterly arbitrary.

In the case of the tax codes, not one citizen in ten million can tell whether he has committed a trivial error or subjected himself to the risk of a felony conviction. In addition, by a grotesque inversion of legal principle, the burden is on the taxpayer to prove his innocence.[55]

Note Meachling's statement that enforcement now is "utterly arbitrary." In the WALL STREET JOURNAL, Circuit Court

---

[55] Reprinted in the SACRAMENTO BEE *Forum*, July 21, 1991.

of Appeals Judge Alex Kozinski writes: "Over the past half-century the idea that the law consists of objective rules has been supplanted" by what he calls "subjectification."

In other words, Judge Kozinski is angry that laws now are deliberately made unclear. The purpose is to widen the power of law enforcers to catch whomever they suspect of wrongdoing. This also makes it impossible for you and me to know if we are breaking the law. Judge Kozinski writes,

> Legislators often find it convenient to be vague and let the courts figure it out. Justice Frankfurter described a cartoon depicting a senator who tells his colleagues, "I admit this new bill is too complicated to understand. We'll just have to pass it to find out what it means."[56]

Chris, many lawyers are trying to do something about our legal chaos. Please remember this the next time you hear someone make an insulting remark about them.

In fact, help them. The next time you are in a discussion with someone about law, government, or economics, ask them, "Have you heard the other side of the story?" Give them these letters.

Uncle Eric

> *"Does America really need 70 percent of the world's lawyers?...Is it healthy for our economy to have 18 million lawsuits coursing through the system annually?"*
>
> —*Vice President Daniel Quayle*
> *August 13, 1991*

---

[56] WALL STREET JOURNAL, January 31, 1989, p. A14.

32

So Why Do We Have
a Government?

Dear Chris,

Now that you've heard the other side of the story about law, power, and government you may be asking why the Founders set up a government at all.

One reason is that, although they understood more about these things than most experts do today, they didn't have as much information. Their data about the origin of government was less complete, and the science of economics was brand new then. The Founders suspected humans are smart enough to get essential services without government but they didn't have proof.

The most important reason they had for setting up a government is simply that they had no choice. Most people believed government was necessary. If the Founders didn't set one up, someone else would.

The best solution was to create a government, then cripple it, and this is what the Founders tried to do. Read THE FEDERALIST PAPERS of Madison, Hamilton, and Jay. They deliberately made the government slow and stupid. They wanted to be governed by a turtle, not a lion. But ever since, the turtle has been working hard to turn itself into a lion.

In Federalist Paper #48 Madison said the Founders hoped to prevent "the tyrannical concentration of all the powers of government in the same hands." The Founders divided the power among the various branches so that "the encroaching spirit of power" of each branch would be directed at the *other branches* and away from the people. In Federalist #51 he said "Ambition must be made to counteract ambition."

This is the main purpose of the Constitution and Bill of Rights. The checks and balances were to keep the government from being efficient so that no matter who got control they would be unable to do much damage. Infighting would keep the government weak.

President Harry Truman knew this. He once explained, "Whenever you have an efficient government you have a dictatorship." Thomas Jefferson said, "I am not a friend to a very energetic government. It is always oppressive."

Why is our government so often dimwitted, slow, and wasteful? Because the Founders planned it that way, thank heavens.

They felt government is, in Thomas Paine's words, a "necessary evil," with emphasis on the evil. In his first inaugural address in 1801, Jefferson said:

> Still one thing more, fellow citizens — a wise and frugal government, which shall restrain men from injuring one another, which shall leave them other- wise free to regulate their own pursuits of industry and improvement, and shall not take from the mouth of labor the bread it has earned. This is the sum of good government.

This attempt to keep the government small and weak was mostly successful for more than 100 years. In 1821 the Federal Government had only 6,914 civilian employees; sixty years later it still had only 100,020. Not until the 20th century did the government's growth become explosive, now exceeding 2,700,000.

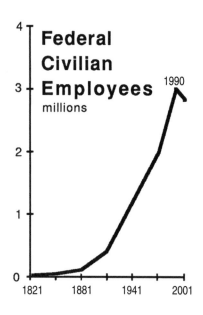

For more than a century, attempts to keep the Federal Government under control were largely successful. Until the income tax and Federal Reserve System were created in 1913, the government was so small and weak it was financed almost entirely through customs duties and taxes on alcohol and tobacco.

Since 1821, the population of the U.S. has increased 30-fold while the Federal Government has increased 390-fold. Now you know why your parents are always complaining about taxes. The turtle has become the lion, and he's hungry.

Interestingly, in 1824 when the Federal Government had about 8,500 civilian employees, Jefferson complained, "I think we have more machinery of government than is necessary, too many parasites living on the labor of the industries." I wonder what he'd say if he could see us now.

Do we need a government at all today? In my opinion, government should be restricted to essential services, meaning indispensable services that cannot be obtained by any other means. If no one has ever found a way to provide an essential service without the use of force on innocent persons, then government should do it.

Of course, we now understand enough about economics to know how to get everything done without the use of force on innocent persons.

Law enforcement, schools, help for the poor, fire protection, military defense, hospitals, you name it, it's all been worked out, tried and proven by someone somewhere by private means. In my next letters I'll give a few examples.

Organizations have been set up to teach how to do all this. You may want to contact:

- Advocates for Self-Government, The Liberty Building, 213 South Erwin St., Cartersville, GA 30120, Ph: (770) 386-8372, www.self-gov.org

- Cato Institute, 1000 Massachusetts Ave. N.W., Washington, DC 20001, Ph: (202) 842-0200, www.cato.org

- Contemporary Economics and Business Association (CEBA), P.O. Box 11471, Lynchburg, VA 24506, Ph: (804) 582-2338, www.summit.org

- Foundation for Economic Education, 30 S. Broadway, Irvington-on-Hudson, New York, 10533, Ph: (914) 591-7230, www.fee.org

- Foundation for Rational Economics and Education, (FREE), P.O. Box 1776, Lake Jackson, TX 77566, Ph: (979) 265-3034, www.nefl.org

- Institute for Humane Studies, George Mason University, 3301 N. Fairfax Dr., Suite 440, Arlington, VA 22201, Ph: (703) 993-4880, www.theihs.org

- Pacific Research Institute, 755 Sansome St., Suite 450, San Francisco, CA 94111, Ph: (415) 989-0833, www.pacificresearch.org

- Reason Foundation, 3415 S. Sepulveda Blvd., Ste. 400, Los Angeles, CA 90034, Ph: (310) 391-2245, www.reason.org

This is not to say we can get rid of all government immediately. It will be a gradual process that could stretch over several centuries. But we must begin now working in this direction or the lion will continue to grow. Soon we will be completely devoured.

Before I end this letter I'll tip my hand a bit and tell you more about my own personal beliefs.

I have faith that all problems can be solved without the use of force on persons who have not harmed someone. I believe this because I believe God did not create a world in which humans must use force on each other.

I believe the world is made so that we always have a choice. The choice might not be clear, but that's why we have been given intelligence, to find the better way.

Consider the alternative. If ignorance excuses the use of force, then the more dimwitted I am, the more force I am allowed to use.

Before the slaves were freed in 1863, no one knew how cotton could be harvested without them. But slavery was wrong and it was abolished, and today cotton is harvested more efficiently than it ever was by slaves. Not only are the blacks better off, but the plantation owners are, too. That's how the world is made. Liberty and free markets not only work, they work better.

Chris, in the following letters I'll give examples of problems that remain unsolved because common law has been destroyed. Until then remember that the Founders were afraid of government and were trying, more than anything else, to set up a government that would do as little harm as possible.

Uncle Eric

"Nothing in fine print is ever good news."

— Andy Rooney
"60 Minutes," CBS

We Cannot Find the Answers

"Man cannot make principles, he can only discover them."
— *Thomas Paine*

Common law was our way of discovering legal principles. Now it is gone, but our high-tech civilization continues moving forward without its guidance. We are left without a rational way to answer legal questions about:

Abortion
Acceptable levels of risk
Animal rights
Artificial intelligence
Assisted suicide
Child theory
Euthanasia
Fathers' rights to children born out of wedlock
Genetic engineering
Irredentism
Ownership of ancient cemeteries
Ownership of archaeological sites
Ownership of extraterrestrial minerals
Ownership of orbits
Ownership of scenic views
Sexuality of mental incompetents
Space junk
Surrogate motherhood
Thermal pollution
Transmission of sexual diseases

33

Unsolved Problem: Risk

Dear Chris,

We are approaching the end of my series of letters about law. In this and the next few I'll give examples of problems that remain unsolved—and that may be unsolvable—because of the absence of common law. We no longer have a rational system for finding solutions; we have only majority rule.

Before we go further, however, I'd like you to do a 3-step mental exercise. First, make a list of all the services government provides. Second, scratch out the ones you believe are not necessary or that yield benefits that are not as great as the costs. Third, try to think of a way the remaining services could be provided without the use of force and without any government involvement—this means especially without taxes.

I believe that with no help you can figure out the answers to at least 90% of them. If you are willing to spend more time on the problem, I'll raise that to 99%.

Few ever do this exercise. I'm sure this is because they've been told by so many government experts that private solutions are not possible.

Now, let's get into some of the more serious problems we have today because of the absence of common law.

One of the worst problems today concerns the question, how much risk is too much? Here's an example.

Suppose I have a gun and I shoot at you, but I'm a bad shot and I miss. I try again, and miss. And again, and again.

Are you allowed to strike back or must you wait until I hit you before you are allowed to defend yourself?

Centuries ago, common law courts held that you didn't need to wait. My first shot—indeed my simple act of pointing the gun and threatening you—was enough for you to take action. I would have raised the level of risk high enough that you'd be allowed to react. I have encroached.

But if I don't threaten you, you can't react. If I'm just holding the gun down by my side and not pointing it in a threatening manner, you can't do anything to me. The level of risk isn't high enough yet.

The key point is the level of risk. In every society people are surrounded by risks of every kind. Life involves risk; we cannot live in a perfectly safe world.

In other words, there is an ambient level of risk. An individual might get hit by a car or caught in a tornado. He might be struck down by a serious disease or die in a plane crash.

We are entitled to take action against others only when they have raised the level of risk beyond the ambient level.

But that's all we know. The common law was gone before judges were able to come up with a definite measure of how much risk is too much.

Can an individual keep a deadly object in his home? Say a chain saw?

Yes, a chain saw is okay. It could fall into the wrong hands and lead to someone's injury or death, but any court would say this risk is not above the ambient level.

Can an individual have a car? Yes, even though cars kill tens of thousands every year, the risk is not excessive.

An electric hair dryer? Razor blades? Matches? Liquor?

Yes, all are dangerous, and some have no redeeming social value at all, but they are within acceptable limits of risk.

In 1991, the Consumer Product Safety Commission released the results of a study about hazards to children.

Between 1985 and 1990, 125 children were killed by drowning in buckets.

Between 1981 and 1991, at least 69 were strangled by drapery cords.

Between 1982 and 1991, 33 children were killed by electric garage door openers. Between 1973 and 1991, 33 were killed by toy chest lids.

Between 1980 and 1991, three lost their lives to the retracting footrests of recliner chairs.

Buckets, drapery chords, garage door openers, toy chests, and recliner chairs are legal. They involve risk of injury or death, but individuals are allowed to have them because the risks are considered within the ambient level.

Can an individual have an atomic bomb?

No, here the risk is too great. A car or a chain saw could kill dozens, but an atomic bomb, if it fell into the wrong hands, could kill millions. Any court would say the atomic bomb is too risky. The police or even the neighbors would be entitled to forcibly enter the person's home and remove the bomb.

But where do we draw the line between the chain saw and the atomic bomb?

At rifles? Shotguns? Thompson submachine guns? Bazookas? Howitzers? Nerve gas?

Where would you draw the line, and why there? I'm sure more Americans have been accidentally killed by drapery cords than by bazookas.

Remember, a rational legal system requires you to have some justification for forcibly entering another person's home and confiscating his property. For us to be permitted to encroach on him, he must first be guilty of encroaching on us, of raising the risk too far.

But we have no way to measure how far is too far. The common law was gone before judges could figure it out.

This is like abolishing the science of chemistry, then trying to discover Teflon. It can't be done.

Another interesting point here is that a shotgun is an extremely lethal weapon. In the hands of an untrained criminal it's far more lethal than the Thompson submachine gun — the famous "Tommy gun." But under political law in most areas of the U.S., the shotgun is legal and the Thompson isn't.

Even among trained police and military commandos, in close-quarter situations, which is where most crime occurs, the shotgun would be the weapon of choice — not the

Thompson.[57] But the Thompson looks more deadly in the movies, which is apparently why it's banned.

In speaking of risk, we must also take into account downstream effects. If we make handguns illegal, some criminals will surely switch to sawed-off shotguns.

Common law was gone before it had a chance to develop tight guidelines to answer questions about risk, and political law is far too crude to have any hope of doing it rationally.

In banning the Thompson and the handgun but allowing the shotgun, lawmakers seem to be saying, "If a criminal shoots someone we want him to use the deadlier weapon." That's political law.

This kind of craziness will continue until the common law is revived and the guidelines on risk are worked out. Until then, all we have is majority rule. We do not know how much risk is too much.

Uncle Eric

---

[57] The Thompson is hard to aim and only makes holes; the shotgun is easy to aim and makes craters.

34

Unsolved Problem: Capital Punishment

Dear Chris,

Another unsolved problem concerns executions of persons found guilty of murder and other especially terrible crimes. Should capital punishment be permitted or should the maximum sentence be life imprisonment?

Should a murderer be drawn and quartered? Boiled in oil?

Some people couldn't care less what happens to a vicious person, but the problem is more complex than that. The desire for revenge is understandable, but look closely at the organization exacting the revenge—the court.

Today's courts are government agencies. Like the post office, the welfare system, and the pentagon, they are not especially well-run. They make mistakes, lots of them. Ask any lawyer.

If we permit courts to order capital punishment, then we are permitting them to accidentally kill an unknown number of innocent persons. Do we want that?

Would you trust your life to the post office?

Furthermore, capital punishment is wasteful. A dead criminal can't do anything to help the families of his victims.

An accountant might point out that the criminal's debt to the family is an asset owned by that family. It's their property. To kill the criminal is to steal this property. It's a violation of the second fundamental law, do not encroach on other persons or their property.

To do anything that keeps the criminal from making payments on this debt is to violate this law.

Under our present legal system, there's nothing we can do about this. The criminal owes his debt to "society" meaning the government. If he kills someone, he has an obligation to make license plates.

Common law had this problem worked out — or at least 95 percent worked out — under the practice of restitution. But that's all gone now. Today, all we have is majority rule.

If you are interested in exploring the question of capital punishment further, take a look at two excellent movies, THE MURDER OF MARY PHAGAN (1988) with Jack Lemmon, and TWELVE ANGRY MEN (1957) with Henry Fonda. As you watch, think how common law could have dealt with these crimes.

And when you talk with someone about capital punishment, ask if they've heard the other side of the story about law, power, and government.

Uncle Eric

35

Unsolved Problem:
The Environment

Dear Chris,

Let's look at a couple of environmental problems. First, the poisoning of the oceans. This is an extremely serious problem because the oceans are the source of most of our oxygen and a large portion of our food. I'll pose a question.

Suppose I dump toxic waste on a farmer's land and destroy his harvest, what will happen?

The farmer will quickly have the sheriff after me.

But suppose I dump this poison in mid-ocean and destroy the tuna the fishermen are trying to harvest. What happens to me then? Probably nothing. Why?

The fishermen are not allowed to have property rights in the ocean. They can't claim an area as theirs, as farmers can on land. The farmer's property rights are protected, and so the cleanliness of his land is protected, but the ocean is unprotected because property rights are unprotected.

Under political law I have as much right to that stretch of water as anyone else does because the ocean is "public property," meaning anyone can use it for anything they please. The same stretch of water can be used for harvesting food, swimming, and dumping garbage.

Here's another environmental problem. You've mentioned your worries about the great Amazon rain forest being destroyed. Each year in Brazil, twenty million acres of forest are cleared.[58] This wonderful source of oxygen, pharmaceuticals, rare animal species, and other benefits is fast being wiped out by Brazilian timber companies and others. Why?

Because the Brazilian government has decided this is in the public interest.

The Amazon lands are not uninhabited. Indians live there and have for centuries. But the Brazilian government asks, How can the property rights of a few thousand Indians be as important as the millions of voters whose jobs require the destruction of this property?

Wherever we find an individual's property rights violated, we find the door open to environmental damage. This is why East Europe and the former Soviet Union are so badly poisoned and filthy. Under their political legal systems until 1990, all land and water were regarded as public property. Whatever belongs to everyone belongs to no one, and no one had much incentive to protect it.

People who wanted to dump garbage in a stream had as much right to do this as others who had always lived on the stream and taken drinking water from it. The legal phrase "in the public interest" led to pollution and poisoning of the public. As I write this today, they remain too poor to clean it up, and it's one of the most polluted areas of the world.

Chris, someday I hope you can travel around the world as I have. You'll see that the nations where the individual's

---

[58] "Empires of the Chainsaws," THE ECONOMIST, August 10, 1991.

property rights are best protected are the cleanest. I've seen ocean beaches, as well as streams, on almost every continent; and everywhere, those that are private are cleaner than those that are public.

So much toxic waste was dumped around the town of Oberrothenbach in socialist East Germany that, unknown to the residents, homes were built of radioactive slag. The water supply is so radioactive it will be dangerous for a thousand years.

All this dumping was held to be in the public interest. Officials asked, how can the property rights of a few hundred villagers be more important than the needs of the nation?

As I said in an earlier letter, when encroachment occurs, the consequences may not be immediately apparent. But they eventually come to the surface somewhere, and they can be devastating.

Few nations today have legal systems capable of providing good protection for an individual's property rights. We have only majority rule, and the majority often votes to trample all over an individual's property. They want the land and water to be public so that they can have easy, inexpensive access to it.

Public property means public pollution. I remember when Yosemite was a grand and beautiful national park. Now it's becoming a filthy city. Yet Disneyland handles dozens of times more people per acre than Yosemite, and it's as clean and fresh as the day it was built. The owners protect their property. They guard the park against vandals, and charge an admission fee that enables them each night to repair any damage done during the previous day.

My personal estimate is that if desirable lands and waters were private property, and if property rights were protected, 95 percent of the world's environmental problems would vanish immediately.

It's a simple principle. You can dump your garbage in your own backyard but don't let the slightest bit — not even the odor — overflow into someone else's.

This applies to noise pollution, too. On your own property you can make all the noise you want, but don't let it overflow above the ambient level onto your neighbor's property. Or, do not encroach. This keeps things clean and quiet automatically.

Uncle Eric

It's an old principle of common law. You can do as you please on your own property but let nothing spill over onto anyone else's. Leave other people's property alone. This keeps the world clean, quiet and healthy.

36

Unsolved Problem: Drugs

Dear Chris,

If government has any legitimate purpose, it's to fight crime. But some Americans believe the government should go beyond this and fight moral corruption. Excessive use of alcohol and other mind-altering drugs are behaviors governments are often asked to fight.

Alcohol is one of the most deadly addictive drugs. It doesn't kill as many people as tobacco, but it's bad stuff. If you know any alcoholics, you know what I mean.

In the U.S. between 1920 and 1933 alcohol was made illegal. Even if a person was not bothering others, he could not have alcohol.

Restaurants and other legitimate businesses were forbidden to sell alcohol. This was the Prohibition Era, and the inevitable black market sprang up. The job of supplying alcohol was taken over by experienced lawbreakers— criminals such as Al Capone.

Capone and other bootleggers would stake out territories to create monopolies. If someone else tried to sell alcohol in these territories, he could be killed.

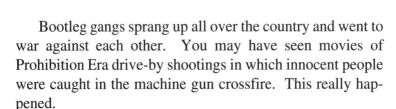

Bootleg gangs sprang up all over the country and went to war against each other. You may have seen movies of Prohibition Era drive-by shootings in which innocent people were caught in the machine gun crossfire. This really happened.

Because alcohol was illegal, the supply and the number of sellers was reduced somewhat, and this boosted the price. Also, the price was made higher simply by the fact that selling was more risky; no one would supply alcohol unless the price contained great profit.

As police intensified their efforts to catch bootleggers, the profit built into the price of alcohol became so high that more and more sellers were created until even children were selling. Hard to believe, but true. Enforcement of the law against selling this drug was creating more sellers.

The quality was poor, too. Once legitimate firms were out of the business, the criminals would sometimes sell liquor that would make a person insane, blind, or even dead.

But alcohol had been made a forbidden fruit, and millions wanted it more than ever. Rebellious teenagers lusted after it, and made big money selling it to their friends. To get the money to buy it, some addicts would steal. The crime rate soared.

After six years of the legal prohibition of alcohol, in 1926, officials at state insane asylums reported the number of demented persons due to alcoholism had increased a thousand percent.[59]

When we encroach on others, even if it's to save them from self-destructive behavior, we set up a chain of events that can lead to deep trouble.

---

[59] CHRONICLE OF THE 20TH CENTURY, edited by Clifton Daniel, Chronicle Publications, Mt. Kisco, NY, 1982, p. 337.

After nine years of Prohibition, in 1929, Metropolitan Life Insurance Company found that deaths from alcoholism among its policyholders had increased six-hundred percent.[60] And, this horrible toll did not include the innocent persons killed by criminals.

Finally Prohibition was repealed, but few seem to have learned much from it. Today, any police officer will tell you most crime is drug related. This is because

> *"Laws provide against injury from others; but not from ourselves. God himself will not save men against their wills."*
> — *Thomas Jefferson*

the price is so high. As I write this, a day's fix that should cost less than five dollars, might cost forty or fifty times as much because of the risk of selling it.

At these prices, the addict can't live on charity or welfare, he must steal. And, to get a hundred dollars cash, he must steal four-hundred or more worth of goods to fence.[61] Every day.

The more the police crack down on drugs, the higher the crime rate goes. Neighborhoods that were once quite safe have become battle grounds. Americans are living under siege. They are afraid to go out at night and they live in homes fortified with security systems, barred windows, and guard dogs.

Again, when the police are instructed to fight immoral behavior instead of crime, the results can be awful. A serious problem has been transformed into a major catastrophe. Thousands of innocent people are suffering for no reason.

We will never get rid of drug abuse altogether. I've long felt an important partial solution is the common law principle of contract voidability. Here's how it could work.

---

[60] Ibid. p. 380.
[61] To fence: sell illegally, usually at much less than the legal value.

Contracts entered into by minors are generally voidable by the minor. This means that the minor can cancel the contract because his judgment may be poor and a shrewd adult could take unfair advantage.

Under common law, if the minor decides to void a purchase, the seller must return his money. The minor is not required to return the merchandise or make reimbursement for it if the merchandise has been used up or destroyed.

In other words, all the risk of the transaction is borne by the adult seller.

Suppose cocaine and other harmful drugs were legal. Under common law, a teenager could walk into a store and buy some, destroy it, and then return to the store for a refund.

A few incidents like this, carefully engineered and supervised by the parent, and any seller of the harmful drugs would be most careful to avoid selling to minors.

Notice that the parents would not need to launch a major political campaign to get the job done. They would not need to organize thousands of voters, or demand that the police spend more money patrolling for drug sellers.

Any parent could get the job done alone because common law judges down through the centuries had already worked out the solution. A minor's contracts are voidable.

At least the price would be lowered so that teens wouldn't find it profitable to push drugs in the schools.

Chris, voluntary organizations such as Alcoholics Anonymous stop more alcoholism in one week than Prohibition did in thirteen years. But voluntarism is the way of the common law, and common law is gone now, we have only majority rule. If the majority wants more crime-causing laws against drugs, that's what we'll get.

The next time you hear someone complain about drugs or crime, ask if they've heard the other side of the story about law, power, and government.

Uncle Eric

37

Unsolved Problem: War

Dear Chris,

Probably the worst unsolved problem is war. In some years, millions kill each other in the ultimate violation of the second law.

We will probably never get rid of war altogether. Some political leader somewhere will do something to stir one up, either openly or secretly. The deceit used to do this can be amazingly persuasive. Jefferson said:

> Never was so much false arithmetic employed on any subject, as that which has been employed to persuade nations that it is in their interest to go to war.

A politician who works all his life to acquire power is understandably eager to use it. He may not fully understand what he is feeling, but he is feeling this.

One of the worst misconceptions that bring wars is collective guilt. Collective guilt is the assumption that if someone does harm, others who took no part in it — who might even have been opposed to it — nevertheless share the guilt.

After Germany lost World War I, the governments of Britain and France decided to make all the German people pay for it, as if all Germans had been in favor of it and all British and French opposed. Collective guilt and collective innocence.

Crushing reparations were levied. Germans had to turn over land, factories, rail equipment, coal mines, and billions in cash to the British and French governments. This demolished the already weakened German economy and impoverished millions of Germans.

The 1920s were terrible for the Germans, and the 1930s brought the Great Depression, which made them even more desperate. Unemployment in Germany hit 40%, one of the highest levels ever recorded in any industrialized nation.

The Germans were desperate for someone, anyone, to help them, and this someone turned out to be Adolph Hitler.

In other words, the British and French governments did as much to cause World War II as the Germans did because they believed in collective guilt. They held all the German people personally responsible for World War I and took revenge against them by stealing property even from Germans who had opposed the war.[62]

Encroachment leads to war. Obvious, right? Well, apparently not for some persons.

Years ago U.S. officials were supporters of the Shah of Iran. They knew the Shah was a dictator whose secret police terrorized Iranians, but they continued their alliance. The Shah claimed to be anti-Soviet. The reasoning was that the

---

[62] For more about crushing reparations and other causes of war, read the Uncle Eric book WORLD WAR I: THE REST OF THE STORY AND HOW IT AFFECTS YOU TODAY by Richard J. Maybury, published by Bluestocking Press, phone: 800-959-8586, web site: www.BluestockingPress.com

Shah was the lesser of the evils—a dictator who murders hundreds isn't as bad as one who murders thousands.

In 1979 the Shah was overthrown by his own people, and these people still hate the U.S. for supporting him. Some engage in terrorism against Americans.

To counter the Iranians, U.S. officials began helping dictator Saddam Hussein in his war against Iran. Again, the assumption was that Saddam was the lesser of the two evils. You know how that turned out.

When we stick our noses into other people's business it leads to trouble. Even when we do it with good intentions. The road to hell...

At one time mankind had a partial solution to war. It was called chivalry, and it was based on the same principles as common law. Today the word chivalry doesn't mean much. A gentleman who opens a door for a lady or helps her with her chair is chivalrous.

Until the 20th century, chivalry meant much more. It was, among other things, a code of honor for soldiers. Chivalry contained a list of persons that soldiers were not allowed to kill. Children, women, the elderly, priests, nuns — and as time passed, this list of protected persons grew longer.

Finally, by the mid-1800s, wars between the more advanced nations had become largely confined just to the military. The civilian populations were often quite safe. In the Civil War, when a battle was about to be fought outside a town, the townspeople would pack a picnic lunch and sit on the sidelines to watch, as if it were a football game.

This is not to say that there weren't many exceptions. Non-combatants were often killed in wars, sometimes horribly and in large numbers. But mankind was moving in the right direction. We had discovered the principle that the deliberate killing of a person who has not harmed anyone is murder—even in war.

In the 20th century, chivalry was trivialized. In most wars now, non-combatants are killed as freely as combatants. In some of the more advanced nations, soldiers sit in underground control centers ready to push buttons that will wipe out millions. These soldiers have been taught there is nothing wrong with this, and they are proud to be ready to do it.

We now have 21st century weapons guided by stone age ethics. We are becoming barbarians with laser-guided bombs.

When the common law disappeared, the moral reasoning behind it went, too. All we have left is the primitive concept of majority rule.

Uncle Eric

38

Unsolved Problem: Irredentism

Dear Chris,

Here's a major unsolved problem that is one of the leading causes of war. It's called **irredentism**, which is from the Italian irredenta, meaning unredeemed.

An irredentist is someone who believes land taken by force should be returned.

This sounds like an easy, straightforward problem. Stolen land should be given back to its owners, right?

If only it were that simple. Should all of America be returned to the Native Americans?

In the U.S., irredentism is little more than an interesting mental exercise because the land will not be given back. But in other parts of the world it's a life and death matter.

Should Israel be given back to the Palestinians?

Should the parts of Poland taken from Germany be given back to Germany?

How about the parts of the Ukraine taken from Poland?

Kuwait taken from Iraq?

Iraq taken from Turkey?

Chechnya taken from Russia?

East Timor from Indonesia?

Endless wars are fought over the problem of irredentism and no one has a solution. How long does a landholder need to keep the land before the original owners lose their rights?

The Israelis and Palestinians have been fighting since 1948, and the Israelis say their right to the land dates back to Biblical times.

No one has a solution to this, and we no longer have a rational way to work it out. The common law is gone, and now all we have is political law, majority rule.

Uncle Eric

Political law is all sword and no principles.

The Effects on Your Career, Business, and Investments

In the March 4, 1989, ECONOMIST magazine, Tom Peters, author of THRIVING ON CHAOS, wrote:

> My first assignment, with McKinsey in the early 1970s, was to evaluate expansion of an agrichemical plant. We ran 25-year cash flow projections. The cost of feedstock for the next 25 years? Simple: the regression line fit for oil prices was tight. Small continuing falls were near certain. Inflation? Habitually a couple of percent, it was a non issue. ... Today one predicts the price of anything — the dollar, a barrel of oil — at one's peril.

We can't plan ahead. Peters doesn't mention it but one reason is because political law has enabled the government to redefine the dollar.

For centuries, "dollar" meant a fixed weight of silver or gold. This definition prevented serious inflation. A government can't create precious metals on a printing press.

In recent decades the law has been gradually changed to allow the government to make a dollar a mere slip of paper with no metal backing. So, like a counterfeiter, the government has been able to print vast quantities of these "dollars" to pay its debts. The value of these paper dollars has been falling, and prices have been rising to compensate.

Legal tender laws force people to accept unbacked paper money as if it were gold or silver. This enables the government to print unlimited quantities of this money, which inflates the money supply. This inflation leads to recessions, depressions, business failures, unemployment, and poverty.

As the inflated money supply sloshes from one area of the economy to another, business managers are led to make more and more mistakes. Business failures become widespread, and unemployment and poverty become fixtures of our society. Millions are stuck in the poverty trap without the slightest understanding of how they got there or how to get out. It's awful.[63]

Under political law, the only business or financial forecast we can make is, present trends will not continue. The best investment advice is, don't get into anything you can't get out of fast, we can't know what the lawmakers will do next.

---

[63] For a further explanation see WHATEVER HAPPENED TO PENNY CANDY?, THE MONEY MYSTERY and THE CLIPPER SHIP STRATEGY by Richard J. Maybury, published by Bluestocking Press, web site: www.BluestockingPress.com, phone: 800-959-8586

39

Unsolved Problem: Poverty

Dear Chris,

In my previous series of letters about inflation, recessions, and investment cycles[64] I wrote about the unsolved
problem of poverty.

Rather than repeal the legal tender laws and go back to a
type of money that cannot be inflated, we've built a giant
welfare bureaucracy to try to make the poor comfortable.

Another cause of poverty was only touched on slightly
by that series of letters. Here's the story.

In recent decades, the tax burden on most taxpayers
around the world has been rising to pay for these giant welfare
bureaucracies. The taxpayers haven't taken this lying down.
They've looked for legal and illegal ways to hide their
money.

An investor can't hide his money by building factories
and office buildings because he can't hide the factories or
office buildings. So, he either spends his money on parties,

---

[64] See WHATEVER HAPPENED TO PENNY CANDY? by Richard J. Maybury,
published by Bluestocking Press, phone: 800-959-8586, web site:
www.BluestockingPress.com

vacations and such, or buys diamonds, art, antiques, gold, and other non-productive assets that are easy to hide. Or he sends the money out of the country to nations where taxes are lower.

This process of hiding money or sending it to safer places to evade taxes is called **capital flight**.

Capital flight means factories, office buildings, and other places of employment are not created. Jobs become scarce. Poverty grows.

Capital flight is the most important reason poor countries are poor. In almost every case, wherever you see hungry and diseased children, you will also find capital flight.

Someone should make a bumper sticker that says simply, "Taxes Cause Poverty."

In 1860, Ralph Waldo Emerson wrote, "In a free and just commonwealth, property rushes from the idle and imbecile, to the industrious, brave and persevering."

That statement could sound harsh and uncaring, as if the poor were poor because they are lazy. If so, read it again carefully. Emerson referred to a country that is free and just.

In an economy where the two fundamental laws are strictly enforced on everyone, including government officials, poverty would be so much less that private charities could cope with it easily. In America, before the Great Depression, they did. In his excellent book FREE TO CHOOSE, economist Milton Friedman wrote that in the 19th century:

> Privately financed schools and colleges multiplied; foreign missionary activity exploded; nonprofit private hospitals, orphanages, and numerous other institutions sprang up like weeds. Almost every charitable or public service organization, from the Society for

the Prevention of Cruelty to Animals to the YMCA and YWCA, from the Indian Rights Association to the Salvation Army, dates from that period.

He also points out that,

The charitable activity was matched by a burst of cultural activity — art museums, opera houses, symphonies, museums, public libraries arose in big cities and frontier towns alike.

When people know that they can save, invest, and plan ahead, and thereby make their own futures secure, they become generous. This is why Americans have always been known as the most generous people on earth. They knew they could afford to be — without putting their own families in jeopardy.

But now the common law principles which made that security possible are gone. All we have is majority rule.

Majority rule leads to arbitrary law, high taxes, and capital flight.

The next time you meet someone who is concerned about poverty, ask if they've heard the other side of the story about law, power, and government.

Uncle Eric

40

Unsolved Problem:
Consumer Protection

Dear Chris,

Every week we read news stories about consumers being poisoned, swindled, injured, and killed by defective merchandise. How can this happen in a nation with hundreds of government agencies and thousands of laws intended to protect consumers?

Chris, the second fundamental law—do not encroach—gets most of the attention, but I sometimes believe the first law—do all you have agreed to do—is more important. This is the law that enables free people to organize themselves.

Extremely complex teamwork, from a boy scout troop to giant corporations, churches, and charities grow from the simple offer, "if you will do this for me, I will do that for you," or "if you will do this for us, we will do that for you."

There are, after all, only two ways to organize an economy: the political way—"do this or go to jail"—and the free market way—"I will do this for you if you will do that for me." Free people use the second way, which requires that promises be kept. Honor.

Consumer protection problems arise when someone doesn't deliver all he promises. Does the toaster toast the bread without burning it? Does it do so for the life of the warranty and without electrocuting the buyer?

Such questions go back to the original agreement — what did the manufacturer promise?

If agreements were enforced, few problems would arise. But the courts today are clogged with cases that have nothing to do with the two fundamental laws, and everyone knows enforcing an agreement can be horribly expensive and time consuming.

Government agencies and political laws that claim to protect consumers work no better than any other part of the government. As mentioned in an earlier letter, governments do not collect taxes to provide services, they provide services as an excuse to collect taxes. The tax is the objective. Once it's collected, the job is done.

But the harm isn't. Because courts can't do what they were intended to do, new agencies and laws are created. All businesses are forced to follow politically created guidelines. This produces a false sense of security among consumers. The old common law warning of "caveat emptor" (buyer beware) is undermined.

Thieves and producers of shoddy merchandise know the government agencies that claim to protect consumers are no more well-run than the post office, they count on it.

These agencies need not do a good job to stay in business. They are tax supported. You are forced to pay for them even if they do not protect you.

In the financial industry, there are horror stories all the time. Investors are offered 25 and 50 percent returns on their money, and they believe this must be legitimate or the government wouldn't allow it. They lose their life savings because they rely on a government guardian angel that doesn't really exist.

Compare this with private consumer protection agencies. Let's take the American Automobile Association (AAA) as an example. AAA rates motels. It doesn't force anything on them, it only gives its opinion of their quality.

The motels request an inspection. AAA checks comfort, convenience, services, and other factors, including cleanliness.

When motels pass inspection, AAA agrees to let them hang a AAA sign out front. I'm sure you've seen this.

These signs have great value to motels and consumers alike. They help increase a motel's business because consumers look for the AAA sign; consumers know the sign means the motel has passed minimum standards.

But AAA goes beyond the minimum. It rates motels on a scale from one to five and publishes directories containing an enormous amount of information to make your selections the best possible. The motels want the highest ratings they can get, so the competition to improve service is fierce. No other nation has a motel industry as fine as America's.

And all of this is voluntary—done by peaceful agreements. No force. It's not perfect, but it works amazingly well, and it's light years ahead of anything the government does.

Also, let me point out that if you want to sleep in a disease-infested firetrap, you are free to do so. In the U.S., however, unlike in most nations, you may have trouble finding one. Free market competition spurred by AAA puts them out of business.

Here's a key point. The fact that AAA can't force anyone to comply with its standards means *no false sense of security is created among consumers*. We all know motels are not forced to comply, so we remain vigilant. Caveat emptor continues to work, and it continues to cause competition to work.

Other private consumer protection agencies include Underwriters Laboratories, which rates electrical goods and other potentially hazardous products, Moody's and Standard and Poors, which rate bonds, A.M. Best which rates insurance companies, and Consumer's Union which publishes mountains of data about products we buy.

Unfortunately, many consumers do not use these protections. They think the government is protecting them. And this false sense of security causes demand for private protection to be lower, so less private protection is available.

I'll finish with my most important point. A private protection agency's *income* is tied directly to its *credibility*. The fewer mistakes the agency makes, the more its rating is believed by consumers and the more it is sought by producers. Producers are willing to pay more for its inspections because its certifications pull in more sales.

But, as I say, private protection is limited because consumers think they don't need it. They think political law is protecting them.

Uncle Eric

41

Unsolved Problem:
Are There More Rules?

Dear Chris,

Are there any rules of behavior beyond the two fundamentals? Certainly.

Be polite.
Be charitable.
Be gentle.
Avoid fatty foods.
Exercise.
Defend yourself.
Read TOM SAWYER.
Keep your house painted.
Wash your car.

Should these rules be enforced in a court of law?
I doubt it. To force these rules on a person would be to
violate the second fundamental rule. It would be encroachment.
My right to swing my fist ends where your nose begins.
I might want to use my fist to force you to be polite or
charitable, but I can't.

To encourage you to be a better person I can use peaceful persuasion, but not force. Force would make me a worse person, and it would probably cause hidden or unhidden damages.

Okay, are there any rules other than the two fundamentals that should be enforced in a court of law?

My best guess is no, but we cannot be certain. I'd like to see religious leaders, philosophers, legal scholars, and economists get together to study the question.

Until then, all we have is majority rule. If the majority wants to punish you for failing to wash your car, they can.

Uncle Eric

The Criminal Justice Museum in Rothenburg, Germany, has a copy of the *Sachsenspiegel*, the common law of the Saxons, which was used as a top law book from 1220 until 1900. It explained how to bring suit, inheritances, property rights, guardianships, and so on. So that illiterate persons could read and understand, each law was illustrated with a picture.

Exhibits in the museum show that German law was especially hard on government officials who were caught committing fraud. In Augsburg, Germany, if the head of the government mint were caught debasing and inflating the coinage, the penalty was loss of a hand. If his inflation amounted to more than 60 pfennings (4.8 ounces of silver, about $25 in today's money) he was burned at the stake.

42

Summary

Dear Chris,

This is the last of this series of letters about law. I think you can see now why I said in my second letter that asking your parents or teachers about common law probably wouldn't help, they weren't taught much about it either.

In a visit to a local high school, I examined six history and civics textbooks. Only three made any mention of common law, and none devoted more than four paragraphs to it. Together they gave it no more than one full page out of a total of 3,851 pages. This for a subject that is very likely the most important we could ever study.

I also checked two law textbooks and they were no better. They mentioned common law only in passing and with the attitude that it's gone now so it's not important, forget it.

Here's a summary of some points you'll want to remember from my letters:

1. An economic system is the result of its legal system. Or, economics is a symptom, the cause is law.

2. The two fundamental laws on which all major religions and philosophies agree are: do all you have agreed to do, and do not encroach on other persons or their property. These laws were the basis of the old common law. But only these two. Except for them we have little or no agreement about right and wrong. There may be other laws, but we don't know. The system for discovering them—common law—was abolished before it could get any farther than these two.

So these are the only laws that can be justly enforced on everyone. To go beyond them would be encroachment.

Since encroachment is forbidden, each person is free to obey other laws if he or she wishes. If, for instance, you wish to obey laws requiring charity, compassion, respect, or something else, no one can rightfully interfere as long as you do not violate the two fundamental laws.

If you meet someone who claims to disagree with these two laws, ask him if he'd like to live in a society where these laws are not obeyed. If he says yes, point out to him that there are many countries where this is the case and all are drowning in poverty.

3. America was the place where the principles of the old common law were more widely obeyed than anywhere else by everyone, including government officials . This is how America became the most free and prosperous land ever known.

4. "All men are created equal," means no one is above the law, not even government officials.

5. Thomas Paine said, "Man cannot make principles, he can only discover them." This is the premise of both science and the common law.

6. There were courts before there was law.

7. The job of the courts was to discover and apply Natural Law. The result was common law, which was the courts' attempt to reflect Natural Law. Common law wasn't perfect, but it was the best mankind has done so far.

8. Natural Law cannot be repealed by good intentions or majority rule.

9. Governments are large organizations that are little different from private organizations. They are made not of angels or miracle workers but of humans who have no special powers or abilities. The only thing that sets these humans apart from the rest of us is that they are not legally equal; they have the privilege of encroaching.

10. Finally, remember the 1946 international court at Nuremberg. The defendants were within their nation's laws, but the prosecution argued that "there is a higher duty" than anything our governments can impose on us. The judges agreed, saying, "The fact that the defendant acted pursuant to order of his government or of a superior shall not free him from responsibility."

Chris, I'm worried that our great country is on a down-hill slide. I cannot imagine anything more important than reviving a scientific legal system in America.

I am reminded of a comment by legal historian Henry Sumner Maine in his 1861 book, ANCIENT LAW. Maine said that in civilizations which have now disappeared, historians find, "the severance of law from morality, and of religion from law, belonging very distinctly to the later stages" of the dead civilizations' legal thinking.[65]

Perhaps the greatest tragedy of our age is that economists do not study law and lawyers do not study economics. Each group makes public policy recommendations that the other group knows are silly or dangerous, but they speak different languages and rarely talk with each other. The crucial connection between law and economics — the connection examined in these letters — remains largely unknown.

When Abraham Lincoln said...

Let reverence for the laws be breathed by every American mother to the lisping babe that prattles on her lap. Let it be taught in the schools, in seminaries, and in colleges. Let it be written in primers, spelling books, and in almanacs. Let it be preached from the pulpit, proclaimed in legislative halls, and enforced in courts of justice. And, in short, let it become the political religion of the nation. And let the old and the young, the rich and the poor, the grave and the gay of all sexes and tongues and colors and conditions, sacrifice unceasingly upon its altars.

---

[65] p.13.

...he certainly was not talking about our insane tangle of political laws. He was talking about common law. But his advice was ignored and today few Americans know what common law is. We must tell them. It's time once again to spread the word.

The place to start is with your friends. Let them read these letters. Ask if they've heard the other side of the story about law, power, and government.

So that they have the whole picture, you might first ask them to read my letters about economics.[66] Also, I suggest you read THE ENTERPRISE OF LAW by Bruce L. Benson. This book contains a plan to return to a completely private legal system, independent of politics.

I'll close by saying we've only discussed the most important points about the connection between law and economics. I haven't covered everything, and I'm sure you have more questions. Please write, I'll do my best to answer.

Uncle Eric

> *"It is the eternal struggle between these two principles—right and wrong—throughout the world. They are the two principles that have stood face to face from the beginning of time; and will ever continue to struggle. The one is the common right of humanity, and the other the divine right of kings. It is the same principle in whatever shape it develops itself. It is the same spirit that says, 'You toil and work and earn bread, and I'll eat it.' "*
>
> *— Abraham Lincoln*

---

[66] Uncle Eric is referring to Richard J. Maybury's Uncle Eric book WHATEVER HAPPENED TO PENNY CANDY? published by Bluestocking Press, phone: 800-959-8586, web site: www.BluestockingPress.com

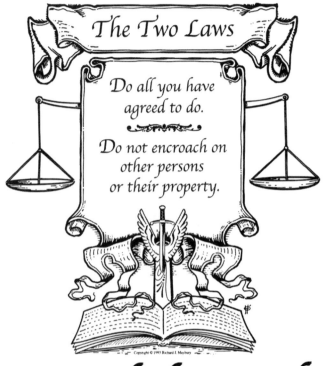

Spread the Word

These are the two fundamental principles of the old British Common Law. They were the original American philosophy — the foundation of the Constitution, Bill of Rights, and Declaration of Independence.

The first law is the basis of contract law; the second is the basis of tort law and some criminal law.

These laws were held to apply to all adults. "All men are created equal," wrote Thomas Jefferson in the Declaration of Independence. Fundamental laws must be obeyed by everyone including government officials; no special privileges or exemptions, not even for the majority.

Appendix

A Memo from Richard Maybury (Uncle Eric)

To Whom It May Concern:

Subject: Restating the two Fundamental Laws

Please forgive my use of a form letter. I've given up trying to handle this on a case by case basis.

Thank you for your interest in the two fundamental laws and for crediting me when restating them.

My formulation of these laws is in these 17 words:

1) Do all you have agreed to do, and
2) Do not encroach on other persons or their property.

Many writers try to compress these laws into less than 17 words. This is understandable. I'd like to be able to do it myself. Some writers paraphrase these laws and then credit me as if their reworded versions are my version.

If you want to do better than my formulation, please give it a try. I hope you do come up with an improvement. But I've been at this for more than twenty years and have chosen each word with great care. My intention is to make the formulation as tightly reasoned as possible so that courts will be forced to see these principles as real, enforceable laws, not as philosophical generalizations.

For instance, I use the phrase "other persons" instead of "others" because I want courts to find a definition for person. This is important for abortion cases and other right-to-life cases. How much intelligence must an organism have to be endowed with a right to life, to be a legal person?

I use the word "agree" instead of "promise." An agreement is a contract, it's binding. A promise may or may not be. And, "agree" assumes the contract is voluntary, not the result of force or deception.

I could go on but you get the point. If you wish to reword the laws, go ahead, but please say you are paraphrasing me—not quoting me. If you do come up with a more tightly worded formulation, please send it along. Many thanks.

—Richard J. Maybury

Comparison

Scientific Law *(Natural Law or Common Law)*	**Political Law** *(Legislation)*

Requirements

Based on fact, logic and the two fundamental laws: 1) do all you have agreed to do, and 2) do not encroach on other persons or their property.	Whatever the powerholders decide.
"All men are created equal"—no special exemptions or privileges.[67]	Whatever the powerholders decide.
Cautious and hesitant in the use of force.	Whatever the powerholders decide.

Characteristics

Predictable, knowable.	Whimsical.
Evolutionary change. Few reversals.	Frequent revolutionary changes. Many reversals.
Discovered by judges, one case at a time.	Made up by politicians in response to political pressure and "influence."
Highly developed, advanced.	Primitive.

Results

Tends to neutralize political power.	Gives powerseekers more power.
Creates liberty and security.	Destroys liberty and security.
Makes effective economic calculation possible—spurs creation of wealth and abundance.	Uses force to redistribute wealth. Destroys incentive to produce wealth.
Stable economic environment.	Boom-and-bust cycles.
Enables civilization to advance.	Destroys civilizations.

[67] Applies to all mentally competent adults, whether acting as individuals or in groups. The problem of children and mentally incompetent adults remains unsolved under both systems.

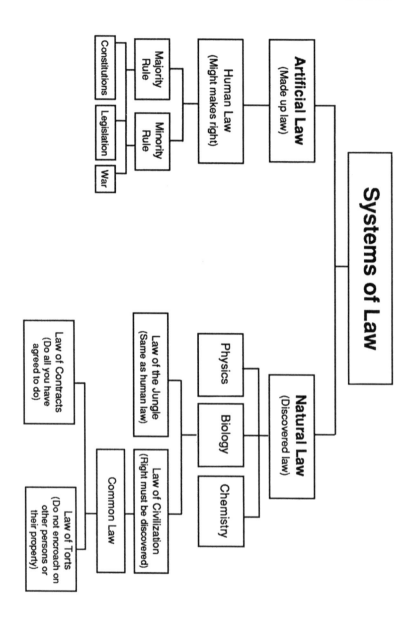

Systems of Law

Artificial Law
(Made up law)

- Human Law
  (Might makes right)
  - Majority Rule
    - Constitutions
    - Legislation
  - Minority Rule
    - War

Natural Law
(Discovered law)

- Physics
- Biology
- Chemistry
- Law of the Jungle
  (Same as human law)
- Law of Civilization
  (Right must be discovered)
  - Common Law
    - Law of Contracts
      (Do all you have agreed to do)
    - Law of Torts
      (Do not encroach on other persons or their property)

Standard of Living *

Of the typical family in the more advanced nations of the time

*Food, cleanliness, lifespan, clothing, housing, medical care and other necessities and luxuries

Interesting exercise: Go through your home and make a list of all the items developed after 1776. Imagine your life without these things.

STANDARD OF LIVING

Arab Moslem Golden Age

American Revolution

America today

Bare survival level

4000 BC	3000BC	2000BC	1000BC	0	1000AD	2000AD

1776

Many students leave school believing civilization has been ascending more or less uniformly since the beginning of history. Not so. Most progress happened after 1776. By any measure, the typical family lived in grinding poverty little better than that of thousands of years earlier until the American Revolution. The fundamental legal principles of 1776 made effective economic calculation possible and these principles spread around the world.

Agreements between Parent and Child or Teacher and Student

The following two agreements are offered as examples; they would probably need some alteration according to the needs of the individual parent and child or teacher and student. "He" should be changed to "she" wherever applicable, and a separate agreement should be written for each child.

The agreements are designed to provide information in regard to the subject matter covered. They are sold with the understanding that the publisher and author are not engaged in rendering legal or other professional services. If legal or other expert assistance is required, the services of a competent professional should be sought.

Agreement between Parent and Child

Preamble

We once had a system for discovering and applying the fundamental legal principles that make an advancing civilization possible. This system was the old common law. Its origins can be traced back at least fifteen centuries but now it is gone.

Before common law was subverted it was able to discover two principles: (1) Do all you have agreed to do. This was the basis of contract law. (2) Do not encroach on other persons or their property. This was the basis of criminal law and tort law.

There may be more principles. We do not know and we no longer have a way to find out.

The two known principles apply to adults only. We cannot be certain to what extent they apply to relationships between children, or between children and adults.

We suspect and hope there are other principles that might guide us in questions relating to children but we cannot be sure what they are.

We do know that children are not well equipped to survive without adult guidance. Also, we believe adults are not entitled to do anything they please to children; a child is not property.

Agreement between Parent & Child

In the absence of guiding principles, we the undersigned agree:

1. We will do our best to work together as a team to make the best of our situation.

2. The parent will do his best to supply the child with adequate food, clothing, medical care, education, and housing. The child understands that none of this is free. Someone must earn it. The child will contribute as much as he can.

3. The parent will give instructions to the child. These instructions will not be arbitrary. The parent will try always to have a good reason for each instruction.

4. The child will follow the parent's instructions, but not blindly. Questions will be expected and encouraged. The child is a thinking person and has a right to explanations.

5. When giving instructions the parent will always make the child's welfare a top priority.

6. If the parent declares an emergency the child will obey instantly. The parent will offer explanations later after the emergency has passed.

7. The parent will try to make all instructions consistent with the two fundamental laws. This will not always be possible but the parent will try.

8. As the child matures, he will be given as much liberty as he can handle. This liberty will always be limited by the two fundamental laws.

9. The child understands that the parent is responsible for the child's actions toward third parties. If the child breaks an agreement or encroaches, the parent must restore the damaged party to his/her original condition. The child is then in debt to the parent.

10. The child will not encroach on others and will fulfill his agreements. To avoid misunderstandings he will always try to make his agreements as clear and specific as possible. Before making an agreement the child will ask, "Exactly what am I agreeing to?"

11. Parent and child will both always try to do what is right regardless of what others do.

12. Many of the parent's instructions will be for the purpose of risk reduction. The child may not have enough experience to understand these risks, and the parent may not be able to explain them. In such cases, the parent will say, "There are risks that you don't know about yet and that I don't know how to explain, please trust my judgment."

13. Many adults do not follow the two fundamental laws. The child will never be instructed to obey another adult unless the parent is absolutely certain this other adult is trustworthy. But the parent could make a mistake. If the child begins to doubt the other adult's trustworthiness, he will immediately do whatever he believes is necessary to be safe and will tell the parent as quickly as possible.

14. The child's first responsibility is to think, and he will not let anyone else do his thinking for him.

15. Eventually the child will reach a stage of maturity in which parent and child both agree that the child is ready for the full rights and responsibilities of an adult. At this stage, parent and child will write an agreement emancipating the child.

16. We will do our best to be patient and understanding with each other. We will always try to see it from the other person's point of view.

17. If we have a dispute about the meaning of a word in this agreement, we will use BLACK'S LAW DICTIONARY to determine the definition.

18. If we have a dispute we cannot resolve, we will choose a neutral third party agreeable to us both to act as a judge. The judge will study this agreement, listen to both sides of the story, examine the evidence and make a decision. We both promise to abide by this decision.

19. We will do our best to obey the spirit as well as the letter of this agreement. Part of this spirit is the nurturing of respect and forgiveness for each other. We will be polite.

20. Every six months we will read this agreement together.

21. This agreement can be changed any time we both agree to the change.

_____   _____

Signature of parent / guardian   date

_____   _____

Signature of child   date

"Honesty, justice, natural law, is usually a very plain and simple matter, easily understood by common minds. Those who desire to know what it is, in any particular case, seldom have to go far to find it. It is true, it must be learned, like any other science. But it is also true that it is very easily learned. ...

"Children learn the fundamental principles of natural law at a very early age. Thus they very early understand that one child must not, without just cause, strike, or otherwise hurt, another; that one child must not assume any arbitrary control or domination over another; that one child must not, either by force, deceit, or stealth, obtain possession of anything that belongs to another; that if one child commits any of these wrongs against another, it is not only the right of the injured child to resist, and, if need be, punish the wrongdoer, and compel him to make reparation, but that it is also the right, and the moral duty, of all other children, and all other persons, to assist the injured party in defending his rights, and redressing his wrongs. These are fundamental principles of natural law, which govern the most important transactions of man with man. Yet children learn them earlier than they learn that three and three are six, or five and five ten. Their childish plays, even, could not be carried on without a constant regard to them; and it is equally impossible for persons of any age to live together in peace on any other conditions."

— Lysander Spooner, attorney, 1808-1887

NATURAL LAW

Agreement between
Teacher and Student

Preamble

We once had a system for discovering and applying the fundamental legal principles that make an advancing civilization possible. This system was the old common law. Its origins can be traced back at least fifteen centuries but now it is gone.

Before common law was subverted it was able to discover two principles: (1) Do all you have agreed to do. This was the basis of contract law. (2) Do not encroach on other persons or their property. This was the basis of criminal law and tort law.

There may be more principles. We do not know, and we no longer have a way to find out.

The two known principles apply to adults only. We cannot be certain to what extent they apply to relationships between children, or between children and adults.

We suspect and hope there are other principles that might guide us in questions relating to children, but we cannot be sure what they are.

We do know that children are not well equipped to survive without adult guidance. Also, we believe adults are not entitled to do anything they please to children; a child is not property.

However, parents are forced by law to expose[68] their children to schooling, and they are forced by law to pay for schools through their taxes. Teachers are unable to offer their services in free markets as other professionals can. And, students' freedoms are limited due to the compulsory nature of the educational laws. The lack of freedom for both students and teachers can poison the relationship between them.

None of this will be solved any time soon, so parents, students, and teachers must work within this system. The purpose of this agreement is to help them do this as humanely as possible.

Agreement between Teacher & Student

In the absence of guiding principles, we the undersigned agree:

1. We will do our best to work together as a team to make the best of our situation.

2. The teacher will do his best to supply the student with a top quality education. The student understands that the teacher can only help, most of the actual work must be done by the student. The student will try as hard as he can. Often this will require him to work even when he does not feel like it.

---

[68] Laws vary from state to state, country to country, and month to month. At any given moment there are places where educating one's own children may be perfectly legal, while in others one may go to prison for it. At various times and in some countries it might even by punished by a firing squad. The only thing we can say with certainty is that political laws change.

3. The student will follow the teacher's instructions, but not blindly. Questions will be expected and encouraged, the student is a thinking person and has a right to explanations.

4. When giving instructions the teacher will always make the student's welfare a top priority.

5. If the teacher declares an emergency the student will obey instantly. The teacher will offer explanations later after the emergency has passed.

6. The teacher will try to make all instructions consistent with the two fundamental laws. This will not always be possible but the teacher will try.

7. The student will be given as much liberty as the teacher believes he can handle. This liberty will always be limited by the two fundamental laws and by the outside rules and regulations the teacher is required to enforce and obey.

8. The student will not encroach on others and will fulfill his agreements. If the student breaks an agreement or encroaches, he must, as nearly as possible, restore the damaged party to his/her original condition. This includes restitution for time lost, emotional duress, and whatever other losses the party incurs. In other words, if a student breaks one of the two fundamental laws, he is creating a debt which he must pay in full.

9. To avoid misunderstandings the student will always try to make his agreements as clear and specific as possible. Before making an agreement the student will ask, "Exactly what am I agreeing to?"

10. Teacher and student will both always try to do what is right regardless of what others do.

11. Many of the teacher's instructions will be for the purpose of risk reduction. The student may not have enough experience to understand these risks, and the teacher may not be able to explain them. In such cases, the teacher will say, "There are risks that you don't know about yet and that I don't know how to explain, please trust my judgment."

12. Many adults do not follow the two fundamental laws. The student will never be instructed to obey another adult unless the teacher is absolutely certain this other adult is trustworthy. But the teacher could make a mistake. If the student begins to doubt the other adult's trustworthiness, he will immediately do whatever he believes is necessary to be safe and will tell the teacher as quickly as possible.

13. The student's first responsibility is to think, and he will not let anyone else do his thinking for him.

14. We will do our best to be patient and understanding with each other. We will always try to see it from the other person's point of view.

15. If we have a dispute about the meaning of a word in this agreement, we will use BLACK'S LAW DICTIONARY to determine the definition.

16. If we have a dispute we cannot resolve, the student will obey the teacher temporarily. Then when time permits, we will choose a neutral third party agreeable to us both to

act as a judge. The judge will study this agreement, listen to both sides of the story, examine the evidence and make a decision. We both promise to abide by this decision.

17. We will do our best to obey the spirit as well as the letter of this agreement. Part of this spirit is the nurturing of respect and forgiveness for each other. We will be polite.

18. Every six months we will read this agreement together.

19. This agreement can be changed any time we both agree to the change.

_____   _____
Signature of teacher   date

_____   _____
Signature of student   date

Thought Provoking Movies
To Spark Discussion About Law

AMERICANIZATION OF EMILY. James Garner. A soldier refuses to participate in the war. Is he right or wrong?

THE CANDIDATE. Robert Redford. An idealistic young man learns how power corrupts.

COUNT OF MONTE CRISTO. Richard Chamberlain. How one man reacts to unjust treatment by legal authorities.

EXECUTION OF PRIVATE SLOVIK. Martin Sheen. True story of the only American soldier to be executed for desertion in World War II. Was he guilty? Of what?

FAREWELL TO MANZANAR. James Saito. Thousands of American citizens imprisoned in desert camps during World War II. Who failed? Why? What's to keep it from happening again?

GUILTY TILL PROVEN INNOCENT. Martin Sheen. True story of a man jailed for a crime he didn't commit.

HARRY'S WAR. Keith Merrill. A man battles the IRS after his aunt is unfairly billed for $190,000 in back taxes.

HIGH NOON. Gary Cooper. A town marshall must face killers alone. Is he obligated to do this when the citizens won't help?

JUDGMENT AT NUREMBERG. Spencer Tracy. The Nuremberg trials and the choices judges made.

LITTLE BIG MAN. Dustin Hoffman. When it was legal to kill Indians, what was a soldier's duty?

ROBIN HOOD: PRINCE OF THIEVES. Kevin Costner. Robin steals from the corrupt sheriff and his followers who have been taking whatever wealth they could from the peasants in the name of law.

SCARLET PIMPERNEL. Clive Donner. Rescuing innocent victims of mob law during the French Revolution.

SEPARATE BUT EQUAL. Sidney Poitier. The Supreme Court searched the Constitution for instructions on segregation and found nothing.

SHENANDOAH. James Stewart. Peaceful farm family is forced to send its sons to a war it doesn't believe in.

STAND AND DELIVER. Ramon Menendez. True story of a teacher using offers and acceptances — agreements — to help barrio high school students achieve amazing results.

THE STAR CHAMBER. Hal Holbrook and Michael Douglas. When the law prevents judges from handing out just verdicts a group of vigilante judges decide to hold their own private court. Classic line from the movie: "Someone has kidnapped justice and hidden it in the law."

TWELVE ANGRY MEN. Henry Fonda. A jury cannot decide if the defendant is innocent or guilty.

Bibliography
and Suggested Reading

Contact your library, order from your local bookstore, or contact the following companies:

Bluestocking Press, web site: www.BluestockingPress.com
Ph: 800-959-8586

Foundation for Economic Education, 30 South Broadway, Irvington-on-Hudson, NY 10533, Ph: 914-591-7230, web site: www.fee.org

Laissez Faire Books,7123 Interstate 30, Suite 42, Little Rock, AR 72209, Ph: 800-326-0996 or 501-975-3650, web site: www.lfb.com

The Liberator Catalog, Advocates for Self-Government, 213 South Erwin St., Cartersville, GA 30120, Ph: 800-932-1776 or 770-386-8372, web site: www.self-gov.org

Liberty Tree Network, 100 Swan Way, Oakland, CA 94621, Ph: 800-927-8733 or 510-632-1366, web site: www.liberty-tree.org

(Contact your librarian for locating out-of-print books).

To get a working knowledge of the basic principles of common law get any high school or college textbook that is an introduction to business law and is based on the UNIFORM COMMERCIAL CODE. Study the sections on contract law, tort law, and property law. This will not be pure common law, but it will be close enough to work well for you on a day to day basis.

To help you develop your own expertise for selecting books that are consistent with the principles of America's Founders, use the guidelines in Richard Maybury's Uncle Eric book titled EVALUATING BOOKS—WHAT WOULD THOMAS JEFFERSON THINK ABOUT THIS? published by Bluestocking Press.

- THE AGE OF REASON by Thomas Paine. Contains much of Paine's thinking about law, government, and philosophy. Published by Prometheus. For ages 16 and up.

- THE AMERICAN TRADITION by Clarence B. Carson. Easy and interesting explanation of America's original philosophy. Fine treatment of Higher Law. Published by Foundation for Economic Education. For ages 14 and up.

- THE ANTI-FEDERALISTS by Jackson Turner Main. An impressively researched examination of the American attempt to stop creation of the Federal Government. For ages 16 and up.

- BLACK'S LAW DICTIONARY by Henry Campbell Black. Definitions of American and English legal terms, ancient and modern. Lots of history. Published by West Pub. For ages 13 and up.

- COMMENTARIES ON THE LAWS OF ENGLAND by William Blackstone. The "bible" for the early Americans' study of law. Difficult reading but worth it. Published by University of Chicago Press. For ages 16 and up.

- THE COMMON LAW by Oliver Wendell Holms, Jr., 1881, 1909, 1923, Little Brown & Co., Boston. "The object of this book is to provide a general view of the Common Law," writes Holmes, and the result is a classic history of the law from Roman times to the present written in layman's language. Must reading. For ages 16 and up.

- THE CONSTITUTION OF LIBERTY by Friedrich A. Hayek. Chapter 11, "Origins of the Rule of Law," and 16, "The Decline of the Law." Excellent history of the discovery of law; ancient Rome, Greece, and the Middle Ages. Scholarly but interesting. Published by University of Chicago Press. For ages 16 and up.

- THE CULT OF LEGISLATION by Phillip Martin Koehne. A 77-page essay about law, legislation and history. Many insights. KDF Inc., 2485 N. Nwy 46, Seguin, TX 78155. For ages 14 and up.

- THE DRINKING GOURD by F.N. Monjo. A wonderful little book about the Underground Railroad and what one man does when legislative law conflicts with Higher Law. Published by Harper. For ages 4-8.

- EARLY CHRISTIAN IRELAND by Kathleen Hughes. Describes early common law systems for law enforcement and care of victims. In many ways these early systems were far ahead of ours today. Published by Bks Demand UMI. For ages 14 and up.

- THE ENTERPRISE OF LAW by Bruce L. Benson. A scholarly, thoroughly researched history of early common law systems, plus a plan to return to a completely private legal system independent of politics. Published by PRIPP. For ages 15 and up.

- EXTRAORDINARY POPULAR DELUSIONS AND THE MADNESS OF CROWDS by Charles Mackay, Harmony Books (Crown), NY. For ages 14 and up.

- THE FEDERALIST PAPERS by James Madison, Alexander Hamilton, and John Jay. The single best collection of writings by three of the most influential Founders. Published by Bantam. For ages 15 and up.

- FREEDOM AND THE LAW by Bruno Leoni. A legal scholar's argument for an immediate return to scientific law. Outstanding. Published by the Institute for Humane Studies. For ages 15 and up.

- THE IDEOLOGICAL ORIGINS OF THE AMERICAN REVOLUTION by Bernard Bailyn. How the early Americans developed a deep understanding of liberty and political power. Excellent. Published by Harvard University Press. For ages 14 and up.

- IT CAN'T HAPPEN HERE by Sinclair Lewis. A novel that shows how an economic crisis could lead to a fascist dictatorship in the U.S. Published by NAL-Dutton. For ages 13 and up.

- IT'S ILLEGAL TO QUACK LIKE A DUCK & OTHER FREAKY LAWS by Barbara Seuling. (Also by Seuling: YOU CAN'T EAT PEANUTS IN CHURCH & OTHER LITTLE-KNOWN LAWS). Examples of ridiculous legislative laws. Published by Lodestar. For ages 7 and up.

- JOURNEY TO JO'BURG: A SOUTH AFRICAN STORY by Beverly Naidoo. Describes what it's like for a black family to live in South Africa and the injustice of Apartheid. Published by Harper. For ages 8-12.

- THE LAW by Frederic Bastiat. In 1850, Bastiat predicted the decline of the law and the subsequent destruction of the economy. Explains the purpose of law. Must reading. Published by the Foundation for Economic Education. For ages 14 and up.

- THE LIFE AND SELECTED WRITINGS OF THOMAS JEFFERSON edited by Adrienne Koch and William Peden. Jefferson was the most insightful of the Founders. This is an excellent collection of his thoughts. Published by Random. For ages 13 and up.

- THE LYSANDER SPOONER READER with an introduction by George H. Smith. Recommended essay on "Natural Law." Published by Fox & Wilkes Publishers. For ages 14 and up.

- MANZANAR by John Armor and Peter Wright. Photographic record of American citizens jailed in desert prison camps during World War II. No one should be granted a high school diploma without first reading this book about the imprisonment of 110,000 innocent Americans in prison camps during World War II. To those who say it can't happen here, this book says it did and it can again. A precedent for the next emergency? Published by Random House. For ages 12 and up.

- NEVER TO FORGET, THE JEWS OF THE HOLOCAUST by Milton Meltzer. The story of Jewish suffering in Nazi Germany, based on diaries, letters, and history books. Published by Harper. For ages 12 and up.

- ORIGINS OF THE COMMON LAW by Arthur R. Hogue. A partial history that contains much valuable information but should be read with caution. Hogue only goes back to 1000 A.D. and makes the surprising claim that common law was "founded" by Henry, duke of Normandy, around 1154 A.D. Published by Liberty Fund. For ages 15 and up.

- THE PATH OF THE LAW by Oliver Wendell Holms. Published by Globe Pequot Press. For ages 14 and up.

- RESCUE: THE STORY OF HOW GENTILES SAVED JEWS IN THE HOLOCAUST by Milton Meltzer. A companion to NEVER TO FORGET. Describes the efforts to rescue Jewish friends and strangers from the Nazis. Published by Harper. For ages 12 and up.

- THE REVOLUTIONARY YEARS edited by historian Mortimer J. Adler. An outstanding source of the original words of George Washington, Thomas Paine, Patrick Henry, and other Founders. History at its best. As I write this today, this book is out of print. Check your local library for a copy. For ages 14 and up.

- THE TRENTON PICKLE ORDINANCE AND OTHER BONEHEAD LEGISLATION by Dick Hyman. Out of print. For ages 12 and up.

- WHATEVER HAPPENED TO PENNY CANDY? by Richard J. Maybury. The first Uncle Eric book and the companion to WHATEVER HAPPENED TO JUSTICE? Explains economics—inflation, investment cycles, recessions, unemployment, poverty, and more. Published by Bluestocking Press. For ages 11 and up.

- YOU'RE THE JUDGE—HOW TO UNDERSTAND SPORTS, TORTS & COURTS by John M. Fotiades. A fun introduction to legal reasoning for the layperson. Uses case histories of sports disputes to illustrate how law works. Although the book accepts the law as it is and does not comment on the validity of legislation, most of the reasoning is according to common law and natural law tradition. An excellent educational tool. Published by Edgeworth & North Books. For ages 12 and up.

Glossary

AGREEMENT. Contract. Two parties in accord or harmony. An agreement always assumes both parties are acting voluntarily without violence or threats of violence. An agreement that is not voluntary is not binding.

AMBIENT. Surrounding conditions.

AMORAL. Without moral sense or principles. Without guidelines for determining right and wrong. Neither moral nor immoral. Also see immoral.

APPEAL. To ask for a legal case to be heard in a higher court which has the ability to overturn the decision of the lower court.

BINDING. Obligatory.

BLACKJACK. A small bludgeon style weapon.

CAPITAL FLIGHT. When investment money needed for creating offices, factories, and other sources of jobs is sent out of the country or hidden. Capital flight usually occurs in response to laws that confiscate money or impair the use of money.

CASE. A dispute between two parties in law court.

CASE LAW. Decisions of judges. Court precedents.

CHILD THEORY. The reasoning underlying laws dealing with juveniles and fetuses. At present, no legal system contains a coherent child theory.

COMMON LAW. The system for discovering and applying the Natural Laws that determine the results of human behavior. The system for discovering and applying the Natural Laws that govern the human ecology. The body of definitions and precedents growing from the two fundamental laws that make civilization possible: (1) Do all you have agreed to do and (2) do not encroach on other persons or their property.

CONTRACT. Same as agreement.

CONTRACT LAW. Law of agreements.

COUNTRY. A geographic area controlled by a government.

CRIMINAL LAW. Laws enacted by governments. Criminal law is usually taken to mean laws against violence, fraud and theft, but in actual fact, governments tend to criminalize anything they don't like.

ECONOMIC CALCULATION. The comparison of costs versus benefits to determine if a gain or loss will occur. The process of an individual deciding if the benefits of a transaction or a job are worth the costs to him.

ECONOMICS. The study of the production and distribution of goods and services.

ECONOMY. The system for producing and distributing goods and services.

ENCROACH. To cross a line. To intrude on the person or property of another.

EQUITY COURTS. Courts of chancery. Courts originally created to make corrections in common law, to place principle above precedent.

FEUDALISM. The political and economic system of small kingdoms in medieval Europe. The king or lord enjoyed near absolute rule over his kingdom and taxed the serfs to whatever extent he pleased.

FORCE. Coercion. The threat or use of violence.

FRAUD. The use of deceit, trickery or cheating to gain unjust advantage from an agreement or transaction. Fraud is usually a form of theft.

FREE TRADE. A voluntary transaction. A transaction in which no one uses force or fraud.

GDP. Gross domestic product. The sum of all final goods and services produced in a nation. Does not include intermediate goods. Example: A car is a final good; the steel it contains is an intermediate good.

GOVERNMENT. An organization that has the privilege of using force on persons who have not harmed anyone.

HIGHER AUTHORITY. A government higher than any human government. God, Nature, the Universe, Brahman, Jehovah, Allah, etc.

HIGHER LAW. A law higher than any human law.

HOMELAND. The territory or region in which a person lives. Can be but is not necessarily a country or nation.

IMMORAL. Having guidelines for determining right and wrong, and choosing wrong. Also see amoral.

INFLUENCE. Peaceful persuasion. The ability to induce cooperation without using violence or threats of violence.

IRREDENTISM. The belief that land taken through force or fraud in the past should be returned to the original owners or the heirs of the owners.

JUDGE. One chosen to decide a case.

JUSTICE. Obedience by everyone, including the government, to the two fundamental laws necessary for a civilization to develop and advance. (1) Do all you have agreed to do, and (2) do not encroach on other persons or their property.

LAW. Broadly speaking, the rules for human conduct which are enforced by violence or threats of violence. More narrowly, law sometimes means common law or Natural Law, as distinct from legislation. "A nation of laws and not of men" means a nation in which the highest law is common law or Natural Law not legislation.

LAWS OF MORALITY. Rules of right and wrong that govern human conduct.

LAWYER. A person trained in the law.

LEGISLATION. Made law, as distinct from discovered law.

LOGIC. The science of correct reasoning.

MORALS. Guidelines for determining right and wrong conduct.

NATION. Same as country. Also see homeland.

NATURAL LAW. The rules that govern the operation of the universe and everything and everyone in it. Natural Law sometimes appears capitalized in the same way as the Ten Commandments.

OUTLAWRY. To be declared outside the law and without the law's protections. A common law concept almost unknown in political law.

POLITICAL LAW. Made up law. Same as legislation. Human law. Might makes right.

POLITICAL POWER. The legal privilege of using force on persons who have not harmed anyone. The privilege of backing one's decisions with violence or threats of violence.

POLITICS. Maneuvering to acquire and use political power. Politics is often misused as a synonym for influence or chicanery, as in the phrase "office politics," but if it doesn't involve force it isn't politics. Politics is from the same Latin and Greek roots as police. Literally, politics is maneuvering to acquire the privilege of using the police.

POWER. Same as political power. See Politics.

PRECEDENT. A court decision which is a guideline for future decisions.

RESTITUTION. Making good for loss or damage. Work or payment done by a criminal to restore the victim as nearly as possible to the victim's original condition. Restitution is a common law concept almost unknown under political law.

SCIENCE. Systematized knowledge acquired through observation, study, and experimentation to learn Natural Law.

SCIENTIFIC LAW. Verbal or mathematical expressions of Natural Law learned through observation, study and experimentation.

SOCIALISM. An economic and political system under which virtually everything and everyone is owned and controlled by government agencies.

SOCIALIST. A person who advocates socialism. Most socialists have good intentions, they assume government agencies will act in the best interests of the governed, not in the best interests of the government.

TACIT. Unspoken.

TORT LAW. The branch of common law dealing with harm one person does to another.

TWO FUNDAMENTAL LAWS. The two laws on which all major religions and philosophies agree. The two laws necessary for a civilization to develop and advance. (1) Do all you have agreed to do and (2) do not encroach on other persons or their property.

WERGILD. Restitution.

Index

Published by Bluestocking Press

Uncle Eric Books by Richard J. Maybury

UNCLE ERIC TALKS ABOUT PERSONAL, CAREER & FINANCIAL SECURITY
WHATEVER HAPPENED TO PENNY CANDY?
WHATEVER HAPPENED TO JUSTICE?
ARE YOU LIBERAL? CONSERVATIVE? OR CONFUSED?
ANCIENT ROME: HOW IT AFFECTS YOU TODAY
EVALUATING BOOKS: WHAT WOULD THOMAS JEFFERSON THINK ABOUT THIS?
THE MONEY MYSTERY
THE CLIPPER SHIP STRATEGY
THE THOUSAND YEAR WAR IN THE MIDEAST
WORLD WAR I: THE REST OF THE STORY
WORLD WAR II: THE REST OF THE STORY

Bluestocking Guides (study guides for the Uncle Eric books)
by Jane A. Williams and/or Kathryn Daniels
Each Study Guide includes some or all of the following:
1) chapter-by-chapter comprehension questions and answers
2) application questions and answers
3) research activities
4) essay assignments
5) thought questions
6) final exam

More Bluestocking Press Titles
LAURA INGALLS WILDER AND ROSE WILDER LANE HISTORICAL TIMETABLE
CAPITALISM FOR KIDS: GROWING UP TO BE YOUR OWN BOSS by Karl Hess
ECONOMICS: A FREE MARKET READER edited by Jane Williams & Kathryn Daniels
BUSINESS: IT'S ALL ABOUT COMMON SENSE by Kathryn Daniels & Anthony Joseph

The Bluestocking Press Catalog
Varied and interesting selections of history products: historical toys and crafts, historical documents, historical fiction, primary sources, and more.

Order information: Order any of the above by phone or online from:

Bluestocking Press
Phone: 800-959-8586
email: CustomerService@BluestockingPress.com
web site: www.BluestockingPress.com